TM

COLLECTOR'S COMPASS™

United States Coins

Martingale™
& COMPANY

Credits

President .... Nancy J. Martin
CEO .... Daniel J. Martin
Publisher .... Jane Hamada
Editorial Director .... Mary V. Green
Editorial Project Manager .... Tina Cook
Series Editor .... Christopher J. Kuppig
Copy Editor .... Allison A. Merrill
Design and Production Manager .... Stan Green
Series Designer .... Bonnie Mather
Production Designer .... Jennifer LaRock Shontz
Series Concept .... Michael O. Campbell
Studio Photographer .... Brent Kane
Illustrator .... Brian Metz

Collector's Compass™: United States Coins
© 2001 by Martingale & Company

Martingale & Company
20205 144th Avenue NE
Woodinville, WA 98072-8478 USA
www.martingale-pub.com

Printed in Canada
06 05 04 03 02 01   8 7 6 5 4 3 2 1

Library of Congress Cataloging-in-Publication Data
United States coins.
    p. cm. — (Collector's compass)
Includes bibliographical references and index.
ISBN 1-56477-375-2
    1. Coins, United States—Collectors and collecting—Handbooks, manuals, etc. I. Series.

CJ1832 .A49 2001   2001022226
332.63—dc21

Mission Statement

We are dedicated to providing quality products and service by working together to inspire creativity and to enrich the lives we touch.

CONTENTS

Foreword   4

Introduction   5

Collecting U.S. Coins   7

Essential Background on Coin Collecting   27

Before You Start Collecting   41

Photo Gallery   49

Now That You're Ready to Start Collecting   77

Living with Your Collection   99

If and When You Decide to Sell   107

Resources to Further Your Collecting   111

Representative Value Guide   120

Bibliography and Recommended Reading   123

About the International Society of Appraisers   124

About the Contributors   125

Index   127

FOREWORD

As America's favorite hobby, collecting is exciting, gratifying, and above all, fun—but without the right knowledge, you could be destined for disappointment. Luckily, you've just found the most resourceful and inspiring series of guidebooks available to help you learn more about collecting. The Collector's Compass series approaches collecting in a whole new way, making it easy to learn about your favorite collectible categories—from the basics to the best-kept secrets.

The International Society of Appraisers (ISA) is pleased to be associated with the Collector's Compass series. As the ISA celebrates twenty years of professional education and certification of personal-property appraisers, who currently specialize in more than two hundred areas of expertise, we remain committed to setting the highest standards for our accredited members. The Collector's Compass series of reference books reflects the ISA's dedication to quality and integrity.

Christian Coleman, ISA CAPP, Retired
Executive Director, International Society of Appraisers

INTRODUCTION

Whether it means setting the alarm clock for Saturday morning yard sales, watching *Antiques Roadshow*, or chasing down childhood memories on eBay, collecting has become America's favorite hobby. The joy of finding treasure amid the clutter of a tag sale or a screen full of online offerings is infectious. Who could resist a pastime that combines the fun of shopping, the thrill of the hunt, the lure of a bargain, and the pride of ownership?

Throngs of novice collectors are joining experienced veterans in online bidding and weekend antiquing expeditions. If you count yourself among them, this book is for you.

The editors of the Collector's Compass series realized that today's collectors need more information than what was then obtainable, in an accessible and convenient format. Going beyond available price and identification guides, each Collector's Compass book introduces the history behind a particular collectible, the fascinating aspects that make it special, and exclusive tips on where and how to search for exciting pieces.

Furthermore, the Collector's Compass series is uniquely reliable. Each volume is created by a carefully chosen team of dealers, appraisers, collectors, and other experts. Their collaboration ensures that each title will contain accurate and current information, as well as the secrets they've learned in a lifetime of collecting.

We hope that in the Collector's Compass series we have addressed every area essential to building a collection. Whether you're a newcomer or an experienced collector, we're sure this series will lead you to new treasures. Enjoy the adventure!

In 1964, the John F. Kennedy commemorative half-dollar replaced the Benjamin Franklin design. This example was minted in Philadelphia; thus, no mint mark appears. *Photos courtesy of Rare Coin Galleries of Seattle, Inc.*

COLLECTING U.S. COINS

While some collectibles could be called rare, exotic, arcane, or even bizarre, U.S. coins are right under our noses every day, and in plenty! Who doesn't have some change jingling in his pocket? Yet many of us take money for granted. It's a means of exchange—you give someone a bill, and you get back a handful of coins. You stop to notice only when the design is altered—as is happening right now to our venerable Washington quarter—or when you suddenly realize that the nickel you just pulled out of your pocket has a beaver on it rather than Thomas Jefferson's face. Otherwise, money is all the same to the noncollecting public.

It couldn't be more different for coin collectors. Each coin, while familiar in so many apparent ways, is a singularity. It tells the story of the moment of its making—in heat and under thousands of pounds of pressure. Its faces are marked with the signs of use—scratches, nicks, dents, wear, dirt, and stains. It's covered with symbols and slogans that bespeak our national heritage—from Lady Liberty and Native Americans to presidents and other notables. And it's imbued with historical interest—sometimes intrigue—for those who are inclined to look to the past.

Along with postage stamps and currency (paper money), coins are different from almost all other collectibles. They are issued by

The Saint-Gaudens Double Eagle

Arguably the most beautiful coin the U.S. has ever minted, the original Double Eagle ($20 gold coin) as Augustus Saint-Gaudens designed it was never to see the light of day. First, it took repeated strikes to bring up the full depth of the design, which was both impractical and expensive. More important, the fact that the center design stood higher than the rim meant that it could not be stacked. And because it was thicker than its predecessor, it could not be commingled in the counting boxes then used by banks. Thus, the ultra-deep relief of the pattern was reduced in a redesign. But even this coveted High Relief coin, circulated in 1907, went back for a third redesign later in the year. The example shown is from 1908. *Photos courtesy of Rare Coin Galleries of Seattle, Inc.*

the federal government in a manner highly regulated by statute. They have a recognized face value as legal tender. Coins minted prior to 1965 have a bullion (or "melt") value that fluctuates with the prices of precious metals.

But unlike stamps, whose designs change frequently and dramatically, coins stay the same for long periods of time. Indeed, the design of a denominational coin (one cent, five cents, ten cents, twenty-five cents, fifty cents, and one dollar) intended for circulation as legal tender can be changed no more often than every twenty-five years without congressional approval.

Because coin designs have been so stable for nearly one hundred years (though several odd denominations and transient designs characterized the U.S. Mint in its early years), coin collectors tend to be specialists, technicians, and researchers. One collector may focus on a particular denomination—the dime, for instance—and attempt to collect an example of every dime ever minted, through all the designs and variations known, with every year and mint represented. That enterprise alone could take years of collecting activity. Another collector may focus on die variations, misstrikes, or proof sets. Yet another may build a collection around the works of a notable engraver, such as Charles Barber, or what many consider the apex of American coin design: the Eagle and Double Eagle ($10 and $20 gold pieces) by Augustus Saint-Gaudens.

The Allure of Coin Collecting

U.S. coins are compelling in a number of ways. For the most part, they're made from metals that have enjoyed consistent appeal throughout human history and have even been invested by some cultures with a variety of magical properties. Coins have a pleasing heft, and many of their designs are stunning examples of the engraver's art. They depict symbols of American patriotism and nationalistic spirit.

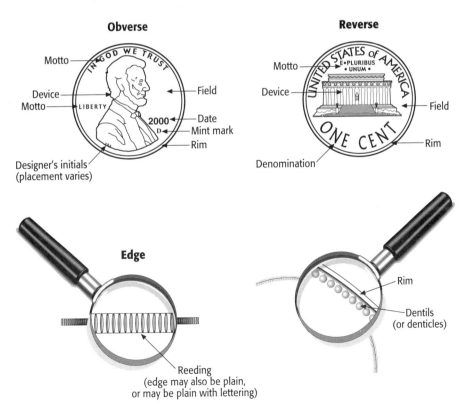

Some collectors are drawn initially to coin collecting by an element of nostalgia—perhaps a childhood memory of Grandpa doling out silver dollars on birthdays. For those inclined to careful study, the attraction is the particular story told by each coin's design, year, and mint mark. A stellar example in uncirculated condition—especially from an early date—has breathtaking impact as a kind of time capsule.

Apart from investors, who are interested primarily in high-grade coins for their monetary appreciation potential, true collectors are turned on by the beauty of coins, the historical details of their issue and use, and nuances of their manufacture. Coin collectors are often driven by a strong organizational impulse to order and complete series and sets. Aficionados of dolls or art pottery are likely to drag you in to admire their collections, but serious coin collectors do not handle their coins very often, do not display them conspicuously, and usually keep them under lock and key in a cabinet, safe, or home vault—or even off premises, in a safe-deposit box. And they aren't likely to discuss their holdings openly, reserving that fellowship and exchange for a trusted circle of dealers and collectors. Depending on the sources consulted, the statistics of participation in U.S. coin collecting vary slightly. But taken together they depict a constituency that's predominately male (88 to 95 percent) and predominately late-middle-aged (average of fifty-two to fifty-eight years old). More revealing is a statistic shared with us by one of the leading publishers in the field, taken from a subscriber survey conducted in 2000, which showed an average expenditure of $2,180 on coins in the preceding twelve months. If you project that annual collecting activity forward in time, over a few years many coin collectors will be amassing collections of considerable value.

Two related crossover categories also attract coin collectors: currency—that is, paper money—and exonumia, which includes a variety of medallic, commemorative, and token material. Exonumia (literally, "outside numismatics") embraces die-struck medals and medallions, commemorative medals cast or struck from precious metals, and tokens (made of metal, plastic, or wood) that historically were, and often still are, used for everything from a beer at a neighborhood tavern to a ride on a trolley, bus, or subway. Like the field of coin collecting, both currency and exonumia are highly organized, with associations, publications, shows, and specialized auctions.

Do You Have the Makings of a Numismatist?

It's relatively easy to become a coin collector. If you want to collect coins in circulation, just go to a bank and buy as many rolls of your chosen coin as you can afford, take them home, and go through them. After you've popped all the needed dates and mint marks into your coin folder or album, you can exchange the remainder for more rolls, and so on. At some point, you're likely to have to go to a coin dealer and pay some premium prices to fill in your key rarities. This kind of collecting can be a satisfying hobby.

But perhaps you're the kind of person who examined snowflakes under a magnifying glass when you were a kid. If so, try this experiment. It's absolutely free, since you can take the coins back to the bank after you've finished.

Buy a roll or two of Washington quarters. First, separate the State Quarters from the others, and divide them by state. If you happened to get a 1976 Bicentennial quarter, separate it out as well. Then organize the rest by date and, within date, by mint mark.

Now get out your magnifying glass and examine the coins for any given year, one by one, under a good light. Look at the obverse (head) first. Note nicks, dents, and scratches in the field areas, as well as the devices (raised areas of the design). Look for wear on the highest spots, tipping the coin from side to side under the light. Perform the same examination of the reverse (tail) of each coin. And don't forget to examine edges. With your naked eye, look at the coins' overall luster—the reflective sheen on relatively unworn coins. Compare them for clarity and depth of strike, keeping in mind that there are subtle differences among individual dies and among stamping presses, as well as in the life cycle of each die's use. Finally, compare the color and toning of the coins. Do some seem more brilliant, while others have taken on a patina of age?

Now choose what you judge to be the strongest, cleanest example for each year. While you may not yet appreciate the technicalities, and may still be learning the vocabulary, you've effectively done a rudimentary grading of your coins. If you enjoyed being able to find the subtle differences that contribute to each coin's uniqueness, you're a good candidate, with study and experience, to become a full-fledged numismatist—by definition, one who studies or collects coins.

Taken at Face Value: The State Quarters Series

The State Quarters commemorative series, initiated in 1999, has precipitated more interest in coins than perhaps any other new issue of U.S. coinage in the twentieth century—attracting more than 100 million collectors, according to U.S. Treasury Department estimates. Even more astonishing, for a tradition that's been so jealously stewarded by the U.S. Treasury and controlled by Congress, is the freedom that's been granted to the states in determining designs and placement of elements on the faces. Although there are some restrictions, each state is allowed to decide how it wants to solicit and select designs, submitting five finalists to the Treasury Department. A committee that includes both the Secretary of the Treasury and the respective state governor makes the final determination of the design.

Compare a State Quarter to a regular Washington quarter. Notice that the denomination and the date have switched positions? The obverse now carries most of the mottoes, with "United States of America" sliding from the reverse, and "In God we trust" moving to the nape of Washington's neck, making way for "Liberty" under his chin. Only *E pluribus unum* ("From many, one") remains on the reverse, fittingly denoting the union of individual states to create the Republic. Convention upon sacred numismatic convention has been overturned by special congressional authorization in the creation of this series!

And what does this portend? Will coins become more like stamps, with new designs introduced frequently? The drumbeats are growing louder for U.S. coinage to be made more interesting and appealing, and the bicentennial of Lincoln's birth, in 2009, provides an obvious opportunity to redesign the Lincoln cent, our longest-running coin. Stay tuned. You may be getting into coin collecting at the most exciting time we've seen in generations.

This series is being struck for general circulation at the Philadelphia and Denver mint branches in standard copper-nickel alloy composition. Proof coins in both the standard alloy version and 90 percent silver are being struck at the San Francisco branch. While the quantities of each circulating version are large—ranging from approximately 660 million to nearly 1.6 billion coins in each of the issues to date—once the minting year is past, no more will be struck.

State Quarters Order of Issue
(following order of admission to the Union)

1999	2004
Delaware	Michigan
Pennsylvania	Florida
New Jersey	Texas
Georgia	Iowa
Connecticut	Wisconsin

2000	2005
Massachusetts	California
Maryland	Minnesota
South Carolina	Oregon
New Hampshire	Kansas
Virginia	West Virginia

2001	2006
New York	Nevada
North Carolina	Nebraska
Rhode Island	Colorado
Vermont	North Dakota
Kentucky	South Dakota

2002	2007
Tennessee	Montana
Ohio	Washington
Louisiana	Idaho
Indiana	Wyoming
Mississippi	Utah

2003	2008
Illinois	Oklahoma
Alabama	New Mexico
Maine	Arizona
Missouri	Alaska
Arkansas	Hawaii

This State Quarters album displays both obverse and reverse behind sliding acetate page covers. Care must be taken when inserting the covers not to create "slide scratches" on the coins. This type of album is fine for storing and displaying circulated coins.

The Coronet design, introduced in 1816, would prove to be one of the most versatile of the nineteenth century. This cent was minted in 1826. *Photos courtesy of Rare Coin Galleries of Seattle, Inc.*

Where to Find Collectible Coins

Collectible coins seldom appear in any significant way in the bottom tiers of the organized secondary market. You won't find fellow collectors hunting down bargains at garage or estate sales and secondhand shops. Once identified as "old," collectible coins usually go directly into the dealer market. From there, they may be sold in shops, at coin shows, in fixed-price catalogs (increasingly supplanted by Web sites), in cataloged auctions held by the major houses, or on numismatic Web sites or general auction sites such as eBay and Yahoo.

The U.S. Treasury occasionally used to dump early coinage from its vaults into circulation, but that practice all but ceased in 1972. A private bank may uncover a hoard of coins, as Wells Fargo Bank did when it found thousands of 1908 "No Motto" Saint-Gaudens Double Eagle pieces some years ago. Those coins went directly to an experienced numismatic dealership, which—through shrewd marketing—kept prices from collapsing as they were introduced into the market.

More rarely, a marine salvage operation strikes gold, as was the case with the recovery of the SS *Central America* in 1989. This treasure ship carried newly minted coins made from gold mined in the California strikes of the mid-1800s. It sank off the coast of the Carolinas in 1857. Again, these recovered coins made their way into the market via high-profile dealerships and auction houses.

Congress abolished the silver dollar in 1873, but in 1878 reinstituted the denomination. Mint engraver George T. Morgan's designs for both obverse and reverse were selected, and the coin, issued through 1904, and again only in 1921, is generally called the Morgan dollar. The example pictured is from 1895, minted in Philadelphia. *Photo courtesy of Bowers and Merena Galleries.*

If you're willing to pay a premium price, you can build a collection of proof sets and noncirculating commemorative coins by purchasing directly from the U.S. Mint. This is more like catalog shopping than collecting, as there's no element of hunting, but an impressive collection of pristine coins satisfies the collecting bug for more than a few numismatists.

Before buying any coin of substantial value, you need to know that grading has become a complex business over the past twenty years. Minute and subtle distinctions are made in the condition and eye appeal of coins that may all appear bright and unblemished to the untrained eye. The difference in value made by one or two grading points can be astonishing.

Third-party coin-grading services authenticate, grade, code, comment upon, and note the variety (if applicable) of a coin, and seal it and its accompanying documentation in hard plastic "slabs." Slabbing coins is the best means known to ensure that a coin and its grading remain paired for perpetuity. The practice has changed the way coin dealers do business with each other, and it's also had an impact on the way coins are collected. With increasing numbers of desirable coins being slabbed, building a collection is more and more a matter of determining the concept you want to pursue and the grade level you can afford, then researching the dealers selling these coins. You need to develop relationships of mutual trust with a few knowledgeable and reputable dealers, and

The Barber quarter was issued 1892–1916; this one was minted in 1905 in Philadelphia. *Photo courtesy of Bowers and Merena Galleries.*

study up on values, grading, and other technical issues with the most reliable books, before you begin your quest in earnest. As one expert counsels new collectors: focus your interests; build a collection that shows care and taste; invest early in one or a few key coins, the ones most desirable and hard to find; and buy the highest-quality coins you can afford.

Ways to Plan and Organize Coin Collections

Numismatists often customize their collections to coincide with their interest in a particular historic period or a fascination with technical production details. You'll want to devise a collecting strategy that focuses on the things that attracted you to the hobby in the first place. Here are some of the common and uncommon ways that devotees have built collections.

By Mint Mark

The U.S. Mint, whose offices are located in Washington, D.C., is the only source for our national coinage, but there are three mint branches (San Francisco, Denver, and West Point) in addition to the headquarters mint, in Philadelphia. Each has its own mint mark. There have been more branch mints in times past. (See "Mint Marks" on page 30.)

By Engraver or Artist

Noted U.S. Mint designers and engravers provide the impetus for some coin buffs. A fine collection can be built around the work of Charles Barber or James Longacre, for instance, each of whom designed several coins.

By Design

Extensive collections are often built around a single coin, such as the Mercury dime, by amassing examples of every mint mark and variety for every year in which the coin was struck.

By Series

The State Quarters series provides an immediate and affordable opportunity for collecting by series. The depiction of fifty individual state designs on the reverse of the Washington quarter dollar is unprecedented in American numismatic history, and is attracting tens of millions of new collectors to the hobby.

By Set

Many collectors strive to acquire complete sets, which can be defined in various ways:

- all examples of a particular denomination, all designs, for all years and all mint marks;
- every coin struck in a given year, in all denominations and for all mint marks;
- all known examples of a particular type of coinage, such as the Lincoln cent;
- all examples of coins in a particular theme—such as commemoratives, including the Bicentennial—or that carry a particular image, such as Liberty, Native Americans, or eagles.

A set can be configured in an almost unlimited number of ways. Do some research and come up with your own parameters— but start with a narrow focus so your goals are within reach.

By Other Criteria

Proofs, including sets that are packaged at the mint for collector purchase, are another possibility. As we'll explain in "Essential Background on Coin Collecting" (pages 27–39), proof coins are distinctly different from coins struck for general circulation, called business strikes. You also may want to consider commemorative coins, struck by the U.S. Mint for fund-raising groups and for issues of interest to collectors. People fascinated by technical minutiae will often build a collection around what are collectively called mint errors—misstrikes, double-strikes, over-strikes, misaligned dies, "mules" (obverse of one coin type mated with the reverse of a different type), or die variations in design, weight of lettering, position of elements, etc. Again, the number of ways to specialize is large.

The State of the Hobby

U.S. coin collecting is the granddaddy of the American collecting world. While many of today's other popular collecting categories started after World War II, Americans have been collecting their coins since the beginning of the nineteenth century. Notwithstanding this "senior citizen" status, coin collecting is robust and in vigorous health. It scores well on all the indicators traditionally used to measure the health of a hobby, as follows.

Collectors' Clubs and Shows

Coin shows are held in almost every state throughout the year. Many are sponsored by regional and local affiliate chapters of the American Numismatic Association. In addition to the opportunity to study singular coins, buy, and sell, they provide workshops, auctions, and other special events. An ANA membership is the single best way for a new collector to plug efficiently into the world of coin collecting.

Publications

The hobby supports a number of newspapers and magazines, including *Numismatic News, Coin World,* and the ANA monthly, *The Numismatist*—to mention just a few. Likewise, books on collecting abound. In addition to the ANA, which publishes for beginners as well as highly specialized advanced collectors, several commercial publishers offer guidebooks and price guides. "Essential Background on Coin Collecting" will recommend some of the "must" publications to get you started.

Established Businesses

A number of nationally recognized auction houses specialize in coins and currency: Heritage Numismatic Auctions of Dallas; Bowers and Merena Galleries of Wolfeboro, New Hampshire; Superior Galleries of Los Angeles; and Stack's of New York, among others. Many dealerships also operate with national and interna-

Coin World weekly and *Coin World Guide to U.S. Coins, Prices, and Value Trends*, 2001

tional recognition. There are hundreds of local coin shops and certified appraisal services, and third-party coin grading services have become a mainstay of the hobby in the past two decades.

Web Traffic and Online Auctions

The Internet has brought about an explosion of information and exchange in the coin-collecting world, as in so many other areas. The ANA maintains an extensive educational Web site, and others are sponsored by the dedicated magazine and book publishers. A tremendous amount of free information is available.

And large auction sites, such as eBay, offer thousands upon thousands of coins for sale each day. Just do a keyword search on a year, say "1898," to see hundreds of coins for auction. More specific keyword searches for special interests—such as "Morgan dollar"—will be similarly rewarding.

New Collectors

The U.S. Treasury Department estimates that the State Quarters series has introduced more than 100 million newcomers to coin

Commemorative Coins

Since 1892 (with a hiatus from 1954 to 1982), the U.S. Mint has produced hundreds of special commemorative coins. These coins have the same denominations as circulating coins—mostly half-dollars—and they are legal tender. However, the designs are unique to each issue. Commemorative designs have recognized individuals important in the history of the nation and celebrated noteworthy events, milestones, and anniversaries. They have also been struck to help pay for memorials of various kinds.

Congress authorizes commemoratives, which are then designed and struck by the Mint. They are sold at premium prices over face value to the collecting market, and a surcharge designated by the authorizing legislation is paid to the sponsoring organization or beneficiary. Historically, unsold coins have been melted.

Commemoratives have also been issued as regular circulating coinage. Some examples are the 1909 cent commemorating the centennial of Lincoln's birth, the 1932 quarter commemorating the bicentennial of Washington's birth, and the 1976 U.S. Bicentennial issues of the quarter, half-dollar, and dollar.

Silver dollar commemorating the 1996 Centennial Olympics (Paralympics). *Photo courtesy of the U.S. Mint.*

The 1893 Columbian Exposition half-dollar was the first commemorative. Many others have celebrated statehood anniversaries, the founding of towns and cities, battles, and pioneer trails. Individuals ranging from Washington and Lafayette to Lewis and Clark and P. T. Barnum have been memorialized. Following much controversy over the number and worthiness of commemorative issues, Congress limited new issues to two per year beginning in 1999. However, it violated its own law by approving multiple commemorative programs for 2001.

Commemoratives are struck in very limited numbers, so their scarcity is established at the outset. The modern series (1982 to present) is still available in MS-65 grade for well under $100 in many instances. The earlier series can be much more expensive for coins of similar quality—climbing into several thousands of dollars. Values tend to be volatile, and collectors of commemoratives seem, for the most part, to be interested in the beauty and design of the coins rather than their investment potential.

The U.S. Mint, an agency of the Treasury Department, is headquartered in Washington, D.C. Shown is the mint in Philadelphia. *Photo courtesy of the U.S. Mint.*

collecting—and spawned an industry to market folders, albums, and holders for these coins. To a lesser degree, the minting of the gold-colored Sacagawea dollar has sparked a new generation's interest. Both new issues provide a good opportunity to build a collection for the face value of the item.

Taken together, a widened audience, a highly organized and professional dealer marketplace, active collecting groups, competitive publications, and the availability of tens of thousands of collectible coins, all contribute to the long-term health of the hobby, as well as indicate an upward value trend. Moreover, the long indifference of the U.S. Treasury to making coin designs more varied seems to be changing. The "shock of the new" as fresh designs appear may well garner more interest in coin collecting over the next several years.

Value Trends

What are the marketplace variables that affect coin prices?

Historically, the value of collectible coins fluctuated with the rise and fall in the prices of precious metals. When gold and silver prices hit all-time highs in 1980, millions of antique coins were sold and melted down for their bullion value. As a result, the survivors acquired new rarity, with consequent increases in value.

Conversely, the appearance of a large cache of previously rare coins—coming out of a bank vault, for example—can cause prices to tumble if the market is suddenly flooded.

Renewed interest in particular types of coins will also affect values. When new research is published in one of the coin magazines or guides, collectors may seek out a coin that was hitherto ignored or of only passing interest. Suddenly the coin is hot and prices take off.

Coin values also tend to move in cycles determined by a combination of investor and collector interest. Periodically, a particular coin becomes attractive to both sectors, as happened in the late 1980s with Franklin half-dollars.

At the turn of the new century, collector interest is high, investor interest is relatively weak, and there's a new factor to consider: While the majority of State Quarters collectors will probably be satisfied with the completion of their sets in 2008, some yet-to-be-determined segment of this huge new enthusiast audience will be bitten by the bug and become serious numismatists. The hobby's next generation is being groomed by this long-term circulating commemorative program.

Why make a distinction between investors and collectors?

The coin market is frequented by two types of buyers: investors and collectors. This is not to say that the two are mutually exclusive or that the same coins never appeal to both. But, generally speaking, investors look for the highest-graded coins, regardless of commonness. They're also interested in the speculative value of true rarities. They typically prefer to buy coins that have been professionally graded and sealed in cases. Slabbing ostensibly assures them that the grade of the coin will stay constant, although grading standards have been known to change, especially during periods when values fall because of drops in bullion prices. Coin investors may know little, if anything, about numismatics.

Collectors, on the other hand, value rarity as well as condition, and place a premium on a coin needed to complete a series or set. Collectors may also attach intangible value to a coin that has a unique or particularly interesting history. Naïve collectors may focus on amassing a great quantity of coins—irrespective of condition or rarity. This is more likely to produce a "hoard" than a coherent collection.

COLLECTOR'S COMPASS

Go for the "Key" Coins

Savvy dealers and collectors alike have given us this advice so many times that it sounds like a litany: Decide on a coin, theme, or series that really appeals to you. Then, read up on it and determine which are the key coins—the rarities—and what you're likely to pay for them.

Without the key coins, your set won't really satisfy the collecting bug. And your investment in the common examples will almost never net you a gain if you decide to sell. Completeness and condition (properly, state of preservation) are critical. It's better to settle for lesser-grade key coins at the outset and try to trade up later than never to have them at all.

Can I build a worthwhile collection even if I can't spend a fortune?

Absolutely. There are opportunities to build an interesting collection on any budget.

Coins can still be obtained at their face value—both new and vintage coins remaining in circulation. Satisfying collections can also be acquired using secondary market sources with a modest outlay (in the hundreds or few thousands of dollars) around a number of different organizing concepts or themes. Of course, the same concepts can require a much more substantial investment if you

Fine Quality, Specialization, and Depth

The John L. Pittman collection was auctioned in late 1997 and early 1998. Pittman is widely acknowledged as one of the preeminent collectors of U.S. (and world) coins of all time. His collection was extensive, but—bearing out our advice to new collectors—it was especially characterized by its fine quality, specialization, and depth.

In particular, Pittman collected proof sets of U.S. coins from the 1830s and 1840s, in all three metals in which they were struck—copper, silver, and gold. These sets realized fabulous prices at auction: a complete 1845 proof set brought $687,500. Many examples purchased for less than $100 in the 1940s sold well into the six figures.

choose to build at a higher grade—for example, Uncirculated or Mint State (MS) coins rather than Extremely Fine (EF) or About/Almost Uncirculated (AU). We'll tell you what these grades mean later on.

Are there overheated market segments that I should avoid?

Your best strategy is to resist buying anything at much more than face value until you've spent some time reading and developing an area of interest. Once a particular design or collecting concept has "spoken" to you, do more focused research and study before you begin to buy.

You'll soon learn that coins are more complex, technical, and value sensitive than most collectibles. There are subtleties in grading standards that can increase or reduce a coin's value as a matter of expert opinion. And, because demand is continually high for collectible coins, there's an element of unscrupulousness in the marketplace that you need to avoid.

Is my collection likely to appreciate?

A well-crafted and thoughtful collection will probably appreciate over the long haul. If you purchase and hold onto a coin for its intrinsic interest as a collectible—whether for rarity, condition, design, historical significance, or because it contributes to completing a series or set—this constitutes its primary value. If the price of that coin goes down (and it's likely to fluctuate with the precious-metals market), its value to your collection remains intact. A passion for the coins themselves separates true collectors from investors and speculators—who should rightly fret when the market value of their holdings nosedives in the short term.

Coin collecting offers continuing rewards and satisfactions for those who are willing to arm themselves with knowledge. Even the casual collector of common Lincoln cents can have a great time with a relatively small risk.

A Coronet Double Eagle ($20 gold piece), commonly called a "Lib 20," issued 1850–1907. This 1857 example was minted at the San Francisco branch. *Photos courtesy of Bowers and Merena Galleries.*

ESSENTIAL BACKGROUND ON COIN COLLECTING

A Brief Look at the Fascinating History of U.S. Coins

The use of coins as a medium of exchange in the geographical area that eventually became the United States of America dates to the earliest Colonial times. Settlers used various items (such as shells, beads, skins, and tobacco) in trade with the Native Americans. But to trade with outside parties, a variety of European coins were commonly employed—English, French, Dutch, German, and Spanish Colonial coins. The Spanish milled dollar—renowned in pirate lore as the "piece of eight" (eight reales in value)—was universally recognized throughout the Colonial period as legal tender, continuing right up to the middle of the nineteenth century!

The first coin minted (rather than imported) in the English colonies was the New England coinage of Massachusetts, in 1652. Following suit, other colonies minted coins and tokens. Individual merchants and traders also had their own tokens and coins struck during the unregulated Colonial period. Incredibly, some of these coins have survived intact: you'll find values listed in the Red Book (the authoritative annual price guide; see "Bibliography and Recommended Reading" on page 123). These rarities, when they appear on the market, most often change hands at elite auctions.

The first coin minted by the United States of America was authorized by an Act of Congress in 1787. Benjamin Franklin purportedly designed the copper coins, featuring the legend "We are one," encircled by "United States" and bordered by a ring of thirteen linked circles representing the original colonies. The reverse depicted a sundial surmounted by a rayed sun: "Fugio" ("Time flies") was positioned to the left, and the date "1787" at right; "Mind your business" appeared at the bottom. These coins were minted in New Haven, Connecticut, from 300 tons of copper believed to have been salvaged from the hoops around powder kegs supplied by the French during the Revolution. These coins are referred to as Fugio or Franklin cents.

Early decisions by Congress defined U.S. coins for the next century. Efforts to depict the first president were resisted by George Washington himself as too imitative of England's monarchical tradition. So, Congress decreed that U.S. coins would feature Liberty on the obverse and the American eagle or another national symbol on the reverse. This decision led to an almost bewildering succession of designs until the appearance of the Lincoln cent in 1909, the first use of a president's likeness.

Heeding the recommendation of then Secretary of the Treasury Alexander Hamilton, Congress in 1792 adopted a decimal system of coinage that prevails—with few past anomalies—even today. The original denominations were:

Gold Eagle	$10.00
Gold Half Eagle	5.00
Gold Quarter Eagle	2.50
Silver dollar	1.00
Silver half-dollar	.50
Silver quarter-dollar	.25
Silver disme (dime)	.10
Silver half-disme	.05
Copper cent	.01
Copper half-cent	.005

The U.S. Mint, an agency of the Treasury Department, was established to maintain exclusive control over the manufacture of coins. It determined the fineness for precious-metal alloys, weights, designs, mottoes, and placement of elements on the faces and rims. The Philadelphia mint made its first coins in 1793.

While American coins were minted for domestic use, they found their way into international trade in large numbers. Indeed, there was a chronic shortage of coins in the early years of the Republic because so much newly minted money almost immediately left the country in trade with international merchants.

Cents and Non-Cents

The names of U.S. coin denominations have been partly a matter of decree and partly a matter of what's stuck, or hasn't, in popular usage. Cents and half-cents have never been officially referred to as "pennies" or "half-pennies" in America. This preference dates from the Revolutionary period, when the uniting colonies were eager to shake off all remnants of things British, including terminology. Nonetheless, common parlance quickly restored the familiar nicknames; even the English slang "coppers" found its way into American use.

The disme and half-disme—derived from the French *dixième* and pronounced "deem"—were "politically correct" because they originated with our allies. However, Americans opted for the more familiar-sounding "dime" and dispensed with the superfluous *s*.

"Nickel" emerged in 1859, with the first minting of the copper-nickel alloy Indian Head cent. A three-cent piece minted in a similar alloy from 1865 until 1889 was also known as a nickel. Eventually, the five-cent pieces first minted in 1866 won the permanent right to the nickname. Interestingly, even the first nickels were made of 75 percent copper and only 25 percent nickel, which is still pretty much the case today.

The slang term "bits" (as in "two bits, four bits, six bits, a dollar") originated with the Spanish milled dollar, accepted as legal tender in the U.S. from Colonial times through 1857. The Spanish milled dollar was worth eight reales, thus giving the quarter, half-dollar, and seventy-five cents their nicknames. In the early nineteenth century the reale was widely used in the American West in place of the dime.

An 1851 Coronet half-cent. This version of the Liberty Head design, issued from 1849 to 1857, shows her wearing a coronet inscribed "Liberty." *Photos courtesy of Rare Coin Galleries of Seattle, Inc.*

Though they were predominantly made of copper, early copper-nickel alloy coins such as this 1866 three-cent piece gave rise to the nickname "nickel." *Photos courtesy of Rare Coin Galleries of Seattle, Inc.*

Mint Marks

Philadelphia was the first location of the U.S. Mint, but eventually it had operations in a number of places. Here's a list of mint marks:

Location	Years Mark Used	Mint Mark
Philadelphia, Pa.	1793 to present	No mint mark until 1979 (except 1942–45 five-cent pieces, marked P); all minting since 1979 marked P
Charlotte, N.C.	1838–61	C (gold coins only)
Dahlonega, Ga.	1838–61	D (gold coins only)
New Orleans, La.	1838–61, 1879–1909	O
San Francisco, Ca.	1854–1955, 1968 to present	S
Carson City, Nev.	1870–93	CC
Denver, Colo.	1906 to present	D
West Point, N.Y.	1984 to present	W
Manila, Philippines	1925–41	M

What materials have been used?

American coins have been minted primarily in alloys of gold, silver, copper, and nickel. The addition of other metals optimizes the results of the minting process and enhances durability. Zinc-coated steel cents were minted in 1943, and from 1942 to 1945, five-cent pieces were made of a copper-silver-manganese alloy, to conserve copper and nickel needed for the war effort.

Both the percentages of precious-metal content and coin weights have varied over the years. All variations were authorized and recorded by the U.S. Treasury Department. The data for any given year's mintage is available in a number of reputable coin guides.

The most dramatic change in metallic composition occurred with the Coinage Act of 1965. This legislation eliminated the silver content from quarters and dimes, and reduced it to 40 percent in half-dollars. Since then, quarters and dimes have been minted in a sandwich: nickel-copper-alloy faces are bonded to a core of pure copper. From 1965 to 1970, half-dollars were made of two faces in an 80/20 silver-copper alloy bonded to a core of 20/80 copper-silver alloy. Since 1971, half-dollars have contained no silver.

Who came up with the designs?

The U.S. Mint controls coin designs and, thanks to diligent record keeping, the identities of designers and engravers have been preserved. This highly accurate and detailed history of coin origins makes the hobby particularly rewarding for those collectors inclined to scholarship and study. For example, the 1909 Lincoln cent carried the initials (VDB) of its designer, Victor David Brenner, on the reverse of some, but not all, coins minted in Philadelphia and San Francisco, thus creating four variations on that year's minting of cents (five, counting the S-over-S mint-mark anomaly).

In many instances, designer-engraver teams created the obverse and reverse faces. Many of these teams were employees of the Mint, but commissions were also given to independent artists, as in the case of the famed American sculptor Augustus Saint-Gaudens. His Eagle ($10) and Double Eagle ($20) gold pieces are arguably the most beautiful U.S. coins ever minted. Coin designs were also chosen in some cases from among entries submitted in competition.

The early designs of U.S. coins bespeak America's idealism and lofty values in the wake of its struggle for independence. Liberty as an allegorical figure could be interpreted in myriad ways. The evolution of her face and figure as envisioned by the exclusively male design staff of the U.S. Mint during the nineteenth century reflects changing ideals of feminine beauty.

For the first hundred years, American coins underwent many changes in design—some sequentially and others simultaneously. It wasn't until 1890 that congressional approval was required for design changes of coins in circulation for less than twenty-five years. This put the brakes on, greatly limiting the character and diversity of coins introduced during the twentieth century. Fortunately, the State Quarters series heralds a change of attitude for the new century.

The Manufacturing Process

The U.S. Mint functions basically as a metal die-stamping factory. Briefly, the design of a U.S. coin originates in a sketch, which goes through stages of oversize modeling in wax, plaster, and resin before a master design is finalized and approved for transfer to die-making machinery.

The master design, called the galvano, is usually several times larger than the final coin. The galvano is placed in a reducing machine that engraves it onto a metal sheet the size of the final coin. The "positive" transfer that results is then heat-hardened. This hardened positive, called a hub, is impressed into sheets of soft steel. These sheets are hardened in turn to create the "negative" dies from which the coins will be struck. The fact that many, many hubs must be created to make the thousands of dies necessary to strike billions of coins leads to opportunities for die errors. Coin collectors place great importance on finding examples of these errors. Values are inversely proportional to the number of error coins struck—the fewer known and the greater the demand, the more valuable they are.

Private-sector companies supply raw materials, manufacturing the metals to government specifications and delivering them in rolled sheets. For alloy-sandwich coins, the metals are bonded by the manufacturers and also delivered in sheets. At the mint, the sheets are passed though a punch press that stamps out rough blanks. These go through processes that weed out bad punches and smooth the surfaces.

Blanks then pass through an upsetting mill that compresses the edges, raising a bead around them. Through precise heating followed by a cold water bath—a process called annealing—the molecular structure of the metal is softened to facilitate its taking of the die image. The fully prepared, but unstamped, blanks are called planchets.

The planchets proceed to an anvil-style die-stamping machine. Each planchet is stamped between two negative dies under pressure, thus creating the obverse and reverse of the coin in one operation. The perimeter of the planchet is simultaneously forced into a third, circular collar die. This die may impress the ridges—or reeding—characteristic on the rims of ten-, twenty-five-, and fifty-cent pieces as well as the dollar. The overall impressing of the planchet is called a strike.

Struck coins are moved out of the machine by conveyor into a hopper that collects them. They are then counted, weighed, and placed into bags or boxes, which are immediately sewn shut or sealed, for their eventual delivery to Federal Reserve banks or private money handlers like Wells Fargo or Brinks.

How Coins Became Collectible

When did numismatics become a formal study?

The American Numismatic Society and the Numismatic and Antiquarian Society of Philadelphia were both established in 1858. The American Numismatic Association was founded in 1891 and received a federal charter in 1912, one of the few organizations chartered by Congress to promote study, preservation, and interest in a collecting field. The ANA charter reads, in part: "The purpose of the organization is to advance and promote the study of coins, paper money, tokens, medals and related numismatic items as a means of recording world history, art, economic development and social changes, and to promote greater popular interest in the field of numismatics."

How did the ideal of preservation become central to numismatics?

A coin begins to encounter wear and damage as soon as it comes into contact with other newly minted coins leaving the stamping press. And that's only the beginning of its ordeal: a typical coin

A 1917 Winged Liberty Head dime, also called Mercury dime. This example was minted in San Francisco. On this type of coin, the bands around the fasces on the reverse are a key element in grading. In the most desirable examples, the three bands are each clearly divided, with high, rounded relief. You'll see this noted in ads as "full split bands." *Photo courtesy of Rare Coin Galleries of Seattle, Inc.*

in circulation undergoes all kinds of use and abuse before an appreciative collector plucks it from its dismal fate—and thus its preservation begins. Such a coin may be professionally graded and sealed in a plastic slab. Even then, the coin may continue to age as atmospheric gases permeate the plastic, and its surface toning may continue to develop.

Coins were—and still are—meant to be used until worn out. They are carried about, passed from hand to hand, shuffled in drawers, run through vending machines, tossed into tollbooth baskets, and rubbed together, nicked, scratched, dented, and dinged, until the federal banks withdraw them from circulation to be melted down—usually after twenty-five years at most.

With so many things working against preservation, it's a wonder that the earliest coins exist at all. During the rapid turnover of coin designs in the nineteenth century, various clever souls must have had the idea to put aside coins that they knew would soon disappear from circulation. Such early "collectors" of American coins likely regarded the coins' intangible value—in addition to their face value and bullion content—as worthy of preservation.

Where can I see examples of these early efforts to preserve coins?

The U.S. Mint maintains exhibits. The Smithsonian Institution has probably the most extensive coin display in the country. And the ANA maintains the Money Museum on the campus of Colorado College. (See "Resources to Further Your Collecting" on pages 117–118.)

Proof of Perfection

Proof coins are struck from specially polished planchets on different presses than are "business strike" coins for circulation. Stringently controlled and exacting processes are used, sometimes creating special surface effects such as mirror or matte finishes. The devices and portrait area of the die may be etched or sandblasted to create the contrast effect known as "cameo frosting" against a mirrorlike field.

Proof coins receive multiple strikes to ensure deep, even images, and to bring up the designs in high relief. These perfect coins never touch each other, and are handled only to be placed into individual protective containers, which are sealed as soon as they leave the stamping press.

Proof set for the year 2000. *Photo courtesy of the U.S. Mint.*

The first proof coins were struck in 1807, as presentation pieces for diplomats and dignitaries. But it wasn't long before the appetites of the collecting market were recognized. Today, the Mint markets proof sets of each denomination minted each year for each branch—at prices considerably higher than face value. The State Quarters series is being minted in a special all-silver edition at the San Francisco branch.

Are proofs a good investment? In truth, the value of most modern proof sets goes down after initial release. Over time, some have appreciated, but it's anyone's guess which sets will become the desirable ones.

By the way, a proof coin is always a proof coin, whether it stays in its original mounting or not. Some proofs do get into general circulation because collectors cut apart the mountings or even use the coins as legal tender if times are tough. The proof coin that's recognized by a dealer or collector may be designated a "PR + number" by a grading service.

EF (Extremely Fine), slight overall wear, designs sharp

F–VF (Fine to Very Fine), moderate overall wear, high points smooth

G–VG (Good to Very Good), heavily worn overall. *Photos courtesy of Rare Coin Galleries of Seattle, Inc.*

Understanding the Perplexing Business of Coin Grading

As a newcomer to coin collecting, you can't go far without encountering its seemingly complex terminology and grading codes. MS-this and AU-that will keep you perplexed until you take time to familiarize yourself with the letter-number combinations used to classify coins, and see and handle many coins in various grades at shows or shops. Suddenly, it will all make sense and you will be able to talk comfortably with dealers and other collectors.

First, plant one concept firmly in your head: a set of letter-number designations is widely—not universally—accepted for the grading of coins. Now, here's an almost contrary concept: there is no agreed-upon standard for applying those letter-number designations. Even experts may grade the same coin differently, based on both objective and subjective factors. This is because grading practices are relative. Different grading services are reputed to be more or less conservative. And, depending in part on market conditions, grading overall may be more or less stringent at different times.

As contradictory as these ideas seem, they're the starting point in understanding coin grading. Now, on to the grades themselves.

Coin grading is done on a seventy-point scale first promulgated by the noted numismatist William H. Shelton in 1948. Shelton intended his system to be used for the Large Cents that were his passion. However, the hobby was so eager to adopt a standard for evaluating state of preservation that soon the Shelton system was being applied to all U.S. coins. The definitive reference, which you can buy at almost any coin shop, is the *Official A.N.A. Grading Standards for United States Coins*. It offers a coin-by-coin guide to determining grade, and it's indispensable.

Grading Circulated Coins

Numbers 1–59 are used for coins that have been in general circulation. Toward the low end of the scale is the About Good (AG-3) grade, a coin in heavily worn condition, barely showing design outlines. At the upper end is Very Choice About Uncirculated (AU-58), a coin exhibiting only the slightest traces of wear. Following are descriptions of some other points.

Very Choice About Uncirculated	AU-58	Slightest trace of wear on high points
Choice About Uncirculated	AU-55	Small traces of wear
About Uncirculated	AU-50	Traces of wear on all high points
Choice Extremely Fine	EF-45	Light overall wear on high points
Extremely Fine	EF-40	Slight overall wear; designs sharp
Choice Very Fine	VF-30	Light overall wear; lettering sharp
Very Fine	VF-20	Moderate wear on higher points
Fine	F-12	Moderate to considerable even wear
Very Good	VG-8	Well worn; center details missing
Good	G-4	Heavily worn; outlines visible
About Good	AG-3	Partial dates/lettering worn smooth
Poor	P-1 or 2	Dates and lettering (even outlines) worn smooth but no mutilation (holed, filed, bent, etc.)

These are greatly abbreviated descriptions: the ANA standards offer detail on how to differentiate among circulated grades for individual types of coins. It's worthwhile to compare several grades of the coin you're interested in collecting. Keep in mind, too, that some dealers only price coins and don't provide a grade. Then it's up to you to determine whether the coin is fairly priced considering its state of preservation.

Grading Uncirculated (Mint State) Coins

Because its mandate is to produce coinage quickly and efficiently for the commercial demands of the economy, the U.S. Mint makes no special effort to ensure that coins are in pristine condition when they leave. A coin's trip through the mint is a rough-and-tumble process. The planchet from which a coin was struck may have had hairline cracks, surface pits, or other flaws even before it became a coin. "Bag" or "contact" marks are typical, a result of the jostling that coins get as they move through the plant and en route to the Federal Reserve banks. The heavier the coin, the more likely it is to incur bag marks. Thus, silver dollars took something of a beating even before they got into circulation.

The eleven Mint State grades—from MS-60 to MS-70—deal in part with extremely fine points of distinction among relatively minor detractions that individual coins exhibit from the minting process. But, theoretically anyway, Mint State coins have never reached general circulation. The other, less objective qualities used to establish the grade of a Mint State coin are luster, strike, and eye appeal (which may or may not include toning).

- **Luster** is the overall sheen that results from the great pressure and heat a planchet endures in becoming a coin. Luster is especially noticeable in the field areas. On large coins, such as silver dollars, the luster may be described as "blast white" quality—referring to a brilliant whitish color—or "cartwheels"—where luster appears to radiate from the center like spokes in a wheel, when the coin is tipped obliquely under a strong light source.

- **Strike** is the depth and clarity of the coin's images. In the most coveted—and highest-grade—coins, lettering and motifs are crisp, and the detail in all aspects is fine. The coin seems to have extraordinary relief depth, a result of having been struck early in the life span of the die. Strikes from the same die, as it becomes worn out, are much less clear and clean.

- **Eye appeal** is truly in the eye of the beholder. Any number of characteristics may cause a grader to push a coin up, perhaps by a full point, because it's especially attractive. For instance, silver coins in various stages of oxidation—called toning— may be particularly colorful and multihued, with concentric or rainbow effects. Or a portrait bust of Liberty may be unblemished, with such excellent depth and detail that it's a standout. Eye-appeal superlatives tend toward the macho among professional numismatists, who talk about "killer" coins, and even "rockets."

The individual descriptive characteristics of the MS-60 to MS-70 grades are too complex to include here. But you should appreciate that the difference in value between coins graded MS-60 and MS-63 may be anywhere from 100 percent to 400 percent—or even greater—depending on rarity.

The Best Resources for a New Collector

American Numismatic Association

The best single point of access to the coin-collecting field is, without question, the ANA. Through it, you can access a variety of materials for study and research, including a wide assortment of guides published by the ANA as well as other publishers.

The membership menu begins with basic adult individual annual dues, with variable rates for longer-term membership, seniors, juniors, and spouses. The ANA publishes a monthly magazine, *The Numismatist*, maintains a research lending library for members' use (reference books circulate to members for the cost of the postage), sponsors a national convention each year, offers educational programs and exhibits, and maintains many affiliate clubs at regional and local levels.

The ANA is headquartered at 818 North Cascade Avenue, Colorado Springs, Colorado 80903-3279; phone 719-632-2646; Web site: www.money.org.

Newsletters and Publications

Numismatic News is published weekly, and *Coins* monthly, by Krause Publications, one of the oldest and most active publishers in the field. *Coin World,* another weekly, has been published by Amos Press for more than forty years. *COINage,* from Miller Magazines, is a third longtimer, published monthly since 1964. With these publications and the ANA's *The Numismatist,* a collector can keep up to date on everything numismatic.

Books

Coin buffs are among the luckiest of collectors, with excellent books available in abundance. The ANA has an active publishing program aimed at beginners as well as advanced, highly specialized collectors. Krause, Amos, Miller, and other commercial publishers offer a wealth of guidebooks on general coin collecting, as well as on specialties and subspecialties.

Then there are the Red Book, the Black Book, and other price guides published in annual editions to track the current values of just about every coin sold in the marketplace. The most useful follow prices over several years. For a close watch on what dealers are paying each other for collectible coins, you can subscribe to the "Greysheet," a weekly price guide.

See "Bibliography and Recommended Reading" on page 123 for a list of titles compiled by our experts to get you started.

One of the two U.S. coins designed by the famous sculptor Augustus Saint-Gaudens, the Indian Head Eagle ($10 gold coin) was issued 1907–33. This example was minted in 1907 in Philadelphia. *Photos courtesy of Bowers and Merena Galleries.*

BEFORE YOU START COLLECTING

You're understandably eager to start collecting, but before you begin to buy, learn as much as you possibly can. Let's begin with guidelines from collectors and dealers who tell you what they wish they'd known when they started out.

The "Golden Rules" of Collecting

1. Buy Quality, Not Quantity

U.S. coins are so diverse that unless you eventually focus on a specialty, your collection will be little more than an aggregation of miscellaneous coins. Once you define your special interest, determine the grade that you can afford by consulting the Red Book or another reliable price guide. Probably a few key coins will be out of reach in terms of availability and/or price. But if you observe the other rules here, your chances increase of finding those desirable pieces over time.

2. Learn Everything You Can

In the beginning, spend as much on books and subscriptions as you do on coins. It's difficult to maintain even a rudimentary involvement in this technical hobby without understanding terminologies, grading systems, the anatomy of coins, and all its other endlessly intriguing facets. Time and money spent on expert guidance will pay you back in useful knowledge, confidence in the marketplace, and awareness of the breadth and depth of collecting possibilities.

3. Collect What You Like

Familiarize yourself with the rich diversity of U.S. coinage, see which coins "speak" to you for whatever individual reasons, and then learn all you can about those particular coins. If you collect the coins that hold fascination for you, you won't regret what you've collected or tire easily of it, regardless of fluctuations in market values.

4. Be Active

Seek out those dealers who are interested in promoting the hobby and getting new collectors off to a good start, as well as in selling coins. They'll share their expertise; you, in turn, will become a repeat customer and recommend that dealer to fellow collectors.

Your membership in a local or regional coin club also provides a forum for information exchange and learning. You'll find a national group as well for almost every area of interest—Early American Coppers, Lincoln cents, silver dollars, and U.S. commemoratives, among many others.

5. Be Patient

With the advent of grading services, more buying is done sight unseen, because people trust both the accuracy of the grading and the guarantee of being able to return the coin. But values—as well as grading systems—inevitably have an element of subjectivity. Whether the coin is at a shop, show, or online auction, if all the factors aren't right, exercise patience and walk away. Another coin of equal or greater appeal will almost always come along.

6. Be Fair

Take pride in conducting yourself in a respectful and generous manner. Building relationships is the key to building a great collection, and collectors reap what they sow. In the long run, your fairness and generosity to others will come back to you many times over.

7. Add to the History

Keep good records of the items you buy. Preservation is central to coin collecting, so always treat the coins in your care properly.

8. Nurture Your Personal Vision

Even if you collect inexpensive, common coins, the energy you put into your collecting can be rewarding for you and evident to others with whom you share interests. For example, the so-called Buffalo five-cent piece, minted from 1913 to 1938, is among the most beautiful coins of the twentieth century. While a few examples have a book value in the tens of thousands of dollars, many in MS-63 condition can be had for under $100, and several more for under $500. If your interest is to collect Fine circulated coins, you can build a wonderful collection for anywhere from $1 to $50 apiece, depending on year and mint mark.

What You Need to Know about the Coin Marketplace

Many of the venues that attract enthusiasts of newer collectible categories are a waste of time for coin collectors. Don't bother with garage, yard, and tag sales. And, although it is within the realm of possibility to find a cache of old coins at an estate sale, it's a hit-or-miss way to spend your "hunting" time.

Flea markets are another favorite of many collectors, but they are not recommended for beginning coin collectors. It's true that larger markets frequently include coin dealers or general dealers who may have a tray or two of coins in cardboard and cellophane 2" X 2" holders. However, the coins are likely to be overgraded, then underpriced (but still priced much higher than actual value) to appear to be bargains. Far worse, they may have been "whizzed"—wire brushed or chemically treated to heighten their shine—or doctored to hide damage or flaws.

You might find coins sporadically at antiques-and-collectibles malls, but they're not likely to be accurately graded or priced. As at flea markets, they'll probably be overgraded, with a "bargain" price attached.

Our panel of experts recommends that you build your collection, at least initially, through reliable and experienced dealers who

COLLECTOR'S COMPASS

More than one of our experts has advocated a "mad money" approach to starting out in coin collecting. Yes, as with any collectible in which you're uninitiated, you should learn first and buy second. But that pent-up excitement usually needs an outlet right away! So, take a modest sum that you can afford to spend indiscriminately, visit a coin shop, and buy an assortment of coins that immediately appeal to you.

Then: Live with them. Examine them. Handle them (carefully, of course, by the edges). See how you feel about them after a week or more. Maybe there's something you begin to like about a particular type that you hadn't really appreciated at first. Or perhaps your initial attraction will cool quickly.

Once you've started to get your bearings, spend some of your available collecting budget on resources to learn more about the coins that hold your interest. If you bought from a dealer who understands how to nurture a new collector, you may be able to exchange some of your first purchases for the coins you've begun to consider your possible focus. You'll likely do more refining during your first months in the hobby, but you're on your way to building a meaningful collection!

know coins and stand behind their merchandise. The ANA counts more than three thousand professional dealers on its member roster. Certified ANA-listed dealers are supposed to abide by a code of professional ethics. For your peace of mind, as well as for building self-confidence, seek out one or more of these as your initial sources.

Here's a rundown of the types of dealerships that specialize in coins, including the ones where you're likely to find high-caliber dealers, as well as the venues you definitely want to avoid.

Individual Coin Shops

A traditional coin shop (sometimes also selling stamps, trading cards, jewelry, watches, or other items) can be found in almost every town of any size. Coin shops rely heavily on the repeat business of local customers—although nowadays, many have Web sites also—and are often a meeting place for coin devotees.

These independent dealers usually advertise that they buy old coins, and they are the ones who are most often called when a cache of old coins is found. They may be mom-and-pop operations where opinions of grade and value are a matter of individual knowledge on both sides of the counter. Or they may be run and staffed by knowledgeable, skilled numismatists who subscribe to the ANA's code of ethics and deal extensively with third-party grading services.

If there are one or more coin shops near you, make a point of getting to know the dealers. Tell them what your interests are, ask questions about their coins, and establish a rapport—your time invested will pay dividends when you start collecting in earnest.

Coins on display at Rare Coin Galleries of Seattle

Web-Based Dealers

On any given day, thousands of coins are available on major auction sites such as eBay and Yahoo (more about these auctions later in this section), as well as from numerous dealers' Web sites. There are also Web rings of coin collectors' sites that offer coins for sale.

In the beginning, stick with established dealer Web sites. These people must build their businesses through satisfied customers, representing their coins accurately and stating payment terms and return policies up front. Other collectors or club newsletters will recommend reliable Web dealers who specialize in your coins—a good way to start.

The downside of buying online is making a decision based on a digital photo or scan, which may not show the coins clearly or may not show all areas, especially the rims. The color, toning, and luster of a coin are difficult to judge, no matter how good the photo is.

Here's a guideline: If you're collecting relatively common, circulated coins of medium grade—Very Good to Very Fine—and if you have the seller's guarantee in writing or via e-mail that you may return the coin if not satisfied, proceed. Ask all the questions you can think of before agreeing to purchase, and examine the coin carefully when it arrives.

If, on the other hand, you aspire to assemble a collection of Mint State coins of any grade, you should buy in person from established dealers whom you know to be reputable. Only if the coin being offered online has been graded and slabbed by a recognized grading service, and the seller offers a money-back guarantee of satisfaction, should you consider buying Mint State coins via the Internet.

Transient Dealers

Transient dealers, also called "vest-pocket" sellers, travel from city to city, visiting coin shops and coin shows. They may buy and sell at shows or from hotel rooms. While there's a reputable element in this tier of the market—dealers who buy for other established dealers, or who sell to a select group of clients—this is also the demimonde of coin dealing.

There are obvious drawbacks to buying coins from someone who is "just passing through." Guarantees of satisfaction may be offered but seldom honored. Because there's a predatory element that counts on the naïveté of coin owners and collectors, this sector is hardly a good place for the beginner.

Telemarketing and Mail-Order Operations

In inflationary times, when coins become attractive as hedge investments, "boiler room" telemarketing operations cold-call people to interest them in buying coins for security in the event of economic collapse. These marketing gimmicks have little, if anything, to do with collecting or responsible investing. The coins are likely overgraded and the prices inflated.

Numismatic magazines carry a variety of ads. Some feature certified coins graded by one of the recognized services. These coins should be delivered to you in a sealed slab, labeled as advertised. Some ads feature coins with formal or informal gradings, but not certified by a grading service. Keep in mind that because all grading is somewhat subjective, you may take issue with the seller's description of a particular coin once it's in your hands.

Apart from offerings of individual coins, you're bound to see ads for starter sets, mixed dates of particular types of coins, and even so-called grab bags. While sellers may tout the tantalizing possibility that these bags contain a rarity, our experts advise that almost always the bags have been thoroughly picked over and contain only common examples, many dupes, and mostly coins in negligible collecting condition.

Many telemarketing and mail-order tactics that offer coins "in bulk" are actually a prelude to signing you up for an approval program, in which you get a monthly offering which you must either buy or return to the dealer. You can build a better collection by eschewing such offers for in-person buying, coin by coin. If you live in a remote area, it's preferable to buy from reputable dealers on the Web.

Rare-and-Precious-Metals Dealerships

Another tier of the market deals in rare and precious metals themselves, appealing primarily to investors. Materials range from

Continued on page 65

COLLECTOR'S COMPASS

Coin Etiquette

Even if you can't afford to buy rare coins, you'll want to inspect some closely at shops or coin shows. In addition to the sheer pleasure of examining a beautiful coin, it's an important part of your education to study a variety of examples in person. You'll be welcome to do so if you adopt the good handling habits that characterize someone who knows what he or she is doing and respects others' property.

- Always pick up and handle a coin between your thumb and index finger, touching only the edges, never the faces. Skin oils and perspiration acids can "etch" your fingerprint into the surface. If you know you're going to be handling coins, wear a pair of light cotton gloves (available at most hardware stores) or latex gloves (available at drug and grocery stores).

- Never talk directly over a coin you're examining. Turn your head away when you speak—and, of course, if you feel a cough or sneeze coming on. Even microscopic droplets of saliva and other bodily fluids can stain the surface of coins.

- Always put a pad, a cloth, or other cushioning under any coin you're examining. Veteran numismatists contend that the most valuable coin is the most likely to be dropped, perhaps due to nervousness.

Your good handling habits will preserve the value of your own coins, and you'll be respected for your courtesy throughout the hobby. As one expert puts it: "Treat every coin as though it's *your* coin!"

Photo Gallery

Double die struck 1955
Lincoln Wheat Ears cent.
The error occurred at the
Philadelphia mint.
*Photo courtesy of Rare
Coin Galleries of Seattle, Inc.*

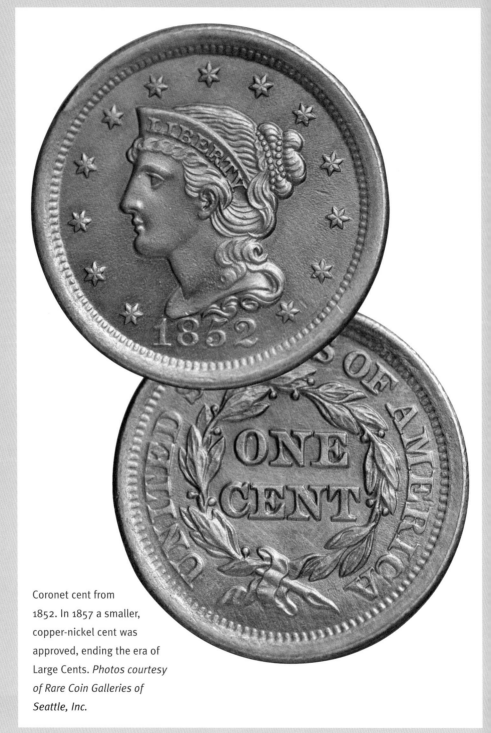

Coronet cent from 1852. In 1857 a smaller, copper-nickel cent was approved, ending the era of Large Cents. *Photos courtesy of Rare Coin Galleries of Seattle, Inc.*

When the Large Cent was abandoned in 1857 (the date of this example), a flying eagle was placed on the obverse of the new smaller coins. This was the only time an eagle would appear on the cent. In 1859 the obverse was changed to an Indian Head design. *Photos courtesy of Rare Coin Galleries of Seattle, Inc.*

The two-cent piece (this one from 1868) is one of the four denominations of coinage abolished by act of Congress in 1873. (The others are the silver three-cent coin, the half-dime, and the standard silver dollar.) *Photos courtesy of Rare Coin Galleries of Seattle, Inc.*

The Draped Bust, another version of the changing image of Liberty, appeared on cents from 1796 to 1807. This coin was minted in 1803. *Photos courtesy of Rare Coin Galleries of Seattle, Inc.*

The Classic Head half-cent was issued from 1809 to 1835. This example was minted in the last year of production. *Photos courtesy of Rare Coin Galleries of Seattle, Inc.*

A shield appears on the obverse of the first copper-nickel five-cent coin, issued 1866–83. This example is a proof coin minted in 1883. *Photos courtesy of Rare Coin Galleries of Seattle, Inc.*

A Liberty head design replaced the shield design on the five-cent coin in 1883, the year this example was minted. But because it resembled the $5 gold coin and included for denomination only the Roman numeral V, unscrupulous persons gold-plated and even reeded the edges of the new coins, in order to pass them at one hundred times their value. Word quickly spread about these fraudulent coins, or "racketeer nickels," and the designer, Charles Barber, was ordered to modify the design to include the word "cents." Interestingly, today "No Cents" coins (which were hoarded) are less scarce than "With Cents" coins (which were used extensively and worn out). *Photos courtesy of Rare Coin Galleries of Seattle, Inc.*

A Buffalo five-cent piece from 1914. The coin is considered the most American of U.S. designs because of its two themes. Three Native Americans posed for designer James Fraser, who created a composite portrait. The model for the bison was Black Diamond, a resident of the New York Zoological Gardens. *Photos courtesy of Rare Coin Galleries of Seattle, Inc.*

In 1916, the Winged Liberty Head dime appeared. The coin is popularly called the Mercury dime—even though the Roman god Mercury was male and the figure on the dime is female. The coin shown was minted in 1923. *Photos courtesy of Rare Coin Galleries of Seattle, Inc.*

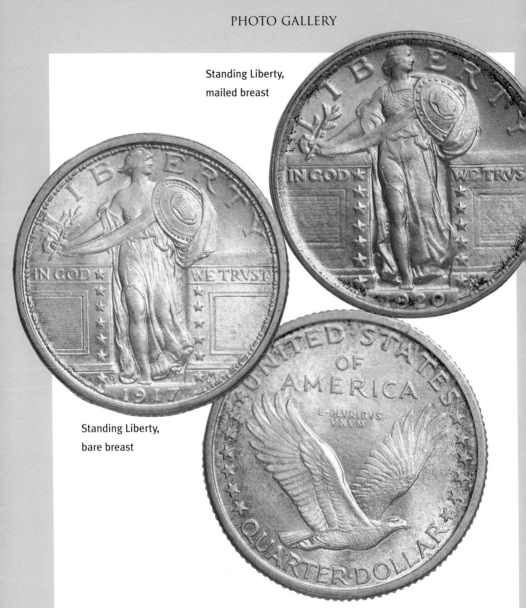

Standing Liberty,
mailed breast

Standing Liberty,
bare breast

The original design of the Standing Liberty quarter (issued from 1916 to 1917 only) shows Liberty with a bare breast on the obverse and no stars below the eagle on the reverse. Some coin histories suggest that there was a public outcry over the "brazen" design, but there's little evidence of it. In fact, it was the subsequent changes to Liberty's garb and the repositioning of the flying eagle and adding of the stars on the reverse which may actually have been illegal, as Congress never approved them. In the altered version of the Standing Liberty quarter issued from 1917 to 1930, a covering of chain mail created a more demure Liberty—and one better cloaked for America's entry into World War I. *Photos courtesy of Rare Coin Galleries of Seattle, Inc.*

A 1938 Walking Liberty half-dollar, issued 1916–47. The eagle on the reverse is considered one of the most attractive on a regular-issue coin. *Photos courtesy of Rare Coin Galleries of Seattle, Inc.*

A portrait of Benjamin Franklin was placed on the half-dollar in 1948, the year this coin was minted, replacing the Walking Liberty designs. *Photos courtesy of Rare Coin Galleries of Seattle, Inc.*

Common obverse

State Quarters Series

While more than ten different animals have been used on U.S. commemorative coins in the past century, Delaware patriot Caesar Rodney's horse is only the third animal, following the eagle and the American bison, to appear on a regular, circulating U.S. coin. South Carolina's state bird, the great Carolina wren, quickly showed up as the fourth in 2000. What other additions to our numismatic menagerie may appear in the State Quarters series between now and 2008?

Delaware, 1999

Pennsylvania, 1999

New Jersey, 1999

Georgia, 1999

Connecticut, 1999

Massachusetts, 2000

Maryland, 2000   South Carolina, 2000   New Hampshire, 2000

Sharp-eyed collectors have already found die errors: on an unknown number of coins, the obverse and reverse sides are misaligned (the top of the design on one side properly should be the bottom of the other). The most valuable examples are misaligned by 180 degrees, so that the designs on both sides are upright when the coin is turned over east to west. *Photos courtesy of the U.S. Mint.*

Virginia, 2000   New York, 2001   North Carolina, 2001

Rhode Island, 2001   Vermont, 2001   Kentucky, 2001

Although the silver dollar was one of the denominations abolished by Congress in 1873, in 1878 a new silver dollar was designed by George Morgan. This example is from 1901. *Photos courtesy of Rare Coin Galleries of Seattle, Inc.*

The Peace dollar, issued 1921–35, was the last silver dollar in general circulation. This coin was struck in 1934. *Photos courtesy of Rare Coin Galleries of Seattle, Inc.*

The Susan B. Anthony commemorative dollar marked the first time that a woman's portrait other than the allegorical Liberty appeared on a U.S. coin. Smaller in size than its predecessors in the denomination, the SBA, as it's known in the numismatic world, was unpopular from the outset because it was so easily confused with the quarter. It was minted only from 1978 to 1981, and again in 1999. *Photo courtesy of the U.S. Mint.*

The Treasury Department's second commemoration of a woman came with the Sacagawea dollar in 2000. The United States Dollar Coin Act of 1997 defined the metallic composition and appearance of this coin, to address criticisms leveled at the SBA. Thus the coin's gold color (a manganese-brass alloy over a pure copper core) and smooth edge, a departure from prior dollars' reeded edges and a point of differentiation from the Washington quarter as well. *Photo courtesy of the U.S. Mint.*

Designs for gold coins became more uniform when the Coronet (sometimes called Liberty Head) was introduced in 1838 for the $10 Eagle, followed by its use on other denominations. The coin shown, struck in 1857, is a Double Eagle ($20 gold coin), issued 1850–1907. *Photos courtesy of Bowers and Merena Galleries.*

The Coronet Eagle ($10 gold coin) was issued 1838–1907. The example shown is from the last year of minting. *Photos courtesy of Rare Coin Galleries of Seattle, Inc.*

The Half Eagle, or $5 gold coin, designed in 1908 by Bela Lyon Pratt, is remarkable for the design feature often incorrectly referred to as "incused." The designs, though in raised relief, are sunk into the surrounding fields so that the highest points are level with the fields. Some claimed that the sunken portions would permit germs to accumulate and constitute a health hazard. This example was minted in 1909. *Photos courtesy of Rare Coin Galleries of Seattle, Inc.*

A 1908 Indian Head Eagle ($10 gold coin), one of the two designs created by the sculptor Augustus Saint-Gaudens, as commissioned by President Theodore Roosevelt. The other was the Double Eagle. *Photos courtesy of Rare Coin Galleries of Seattle, Inc.*

In 1892 chief Mint sculptor-engraver Charles Barber created a new Liberty head for the obverse, and a heraldic eagle for the reverse, of what came to be called the Barber quarter, issued until 1916. This example was minted in 1908. *Photos courtesy of Rare Coin Galleries of Seattle, Inc.*

Continued from page 47

"junk" bags of silver-content coins, priced more or less by weight, to rare, high-quality individual coins in gold, silver, and other precious metals. Dealerships also buy and sell bullion coins and precious-metal ingots. While many of these firms are well established, they are not considered a sector of the mainstream numismatic market.

Coin Shows

Held throughout the country and throughout the year, coin shows sponsored by regional and local ANA-affiliated organizations, as well as by professional show promoters, are without question a worthwhile place to shop for collectible coins.

Offering yet another benefit of membership, ANA-sponsored coin shows generally combine business meetings for club members and officials, educational workshops and seminars, and a bourse. The bourse is a dealer-seller area open to the public where both raw and slabbed coins are offered for sale.

Remember, coin collecting involves a finite number of particularities. So you'll likely find several examples of comparable coins at any given show. If you attend regularly, you will see over and over the specific coins you want to add to your collection.

Dealer Fixed-Price Catalogs and Auctions

The major numismatic galleries—a highfalutin term for big dealerships—conduct live auctions on an ongoing basis. These are advertised in coin publications such as *Numismatic News, Coin World,* and *COINage.* If you call or write for a catalog there's likely to be a charge, but it gets you on the mailing list to be notified of future auctions.

The coins offered here are generally graded by a service or by the gallery's own numismatists. The authenticity of the lots is guaranteed, but the grading is as subject to debate as in other sectors. If you haven't personally inspected the coins during the preview, you're buying sight unseen (relying only on catalog photos) and subject to the rules of the auction (which preclude returns). This is therefore not the place for newcomers to build their collections, although you may find it thrilling and educational to attend a major coin auction as a spectator.

Offers for fixed-price sales lists continue to appear in hobby papers, but increasingly these sellers are migrating to Web sites, where their inventory can be offered for sale twenty-four hours a day, seven days a week, to an international audience without the costs of catalog printing and postage.

Dealing with Dealers

You'll soon discover that reputable, helpful dealers are such an important resource—for valuable information as well as for coins—that it pays to know the ins and outs of working with them. Cultivating relationships with your dealer network will pay big dividends in building a quality collection.

Uncirculated 1969 Lincoln Memorial cent. The 150th anniversary of Lincoln's birth occasioned the change on the reverse of Lincoln cents from wheat ears (1909–58) to the Lincoln Memorial (1959–present). *Photos courtesy of Rare Coin Galleries of Seattle, Inc.*

Can I rely on dealers to know everything about their coins?

Dealer knowledge varies widely. Savvy collectors ask questions—lots of them. When you do, you'll soon get a sense of whether the dealer knows what he's talking about. Specifically, the dealer should be able to give you a context for the asking price. But be prepared to take the time to validate what you've been told before rushing to make a purchase. Your research may disclose that the dealer is in error. That said, it rarely pays to call attention to a dealer's mistake—even when you know you're right. Always remain polite and nonargumentative.

Are most dealers honest?

Fortunately, yes. Dealers who habitually lie to their customers don't stay in business long. But that doesn't let you off the hook: do your homework and ask lots of questions. Dealers aren't out to cheat people, but they can't know everything about every coin that passes through their hands—it's possible to overlook a flaw or make a mistake.

As a new collector, you'll rarely go wrong if you stick with dealers who've built solid reputations. Ask around. And never enter into any major purchase without a written guarantee that notes all pertinent facts about the coin. Any dealer who's unwilling to accommodate you on this doesn't deserve your business.

How can dealers help me build my collection?

Probably in more ways than you can imagine. First, most dealers love to talk about their merchandise, which will give you invaluable insights and information. After all, part of their job is educating buyers about the field they love.

Second, by building a long-term relationship with a dealer you like—by being an active collector who makes regular purchases—you'll earn a spot on his A list. You'll be among the first to be called when truly special items appear on the market.

An additional benefit of a positive rapport with a dealer may be access to his resource library. Many dealers are serious specialists in particular niches of numismatics. It's not unheard of for these dealers to allow trusted customers to use their references, either in the shop or on loan.

Some collectors buy "on approval." What does that mean?

In coin collecting, buying on approval can have two different meanings. We've already talked about the mail-order practice of offering starter sets or mixed bags of coins on approval. When you reply to these ads, you're basically agreeing to allow the dealer to send you coins periodically on approval: within a given period you must either buy or return them.

The other approval arrangement typically applies to dealers sending coins by mail to trusted collectors without payment, but with a prior agreement on price and terms. Here, the dealer is calculating, first, that the collector will appreciate the coin more when he sees it, and second, that the collector will find it easier to send a check than to pack, insure, and return the coin. This is by no means unscrupulous; smart sellers in any business will do everything they can to increase the purchaser's comfort.

Are dealers' prices ever negotiable?

Certainly. Never be afraid to bargain—it's part of the fun of collecting. In fact, most dealers factor a certain amount of "wiggle room" into their asking price—anywhere from 10 to 20 percent.

Just be sure to keep your negotiations positive. Refrain from nagging, or insulting the merchandise. If a piece is slabbed and professionally graded, there's virtually no room for questioning the grade, though the price may be somewhat negotiable. If the seller grades it personally, your challenge may be politely stated as a difference of opinion. It's obviously in your interest to note the flaws you observe, but in most cases neither of your positions is likely to be definitively correct. This is especially true in areas of luster and toning, which are highly subjective.

If you really want the coin but you're adamant about your top price, simply ask, "Would you be open to an offer on this piece?" The more time you invest in your discussion with the dealer, the better your chances of getting the coin at close to your target price. You need to know the market price range for the coin and always counter with a reasonable offer.

If the two of you reach common ground in your negotiations, be prepared to buy. To a dealer, there are few things worse than customers who negotiate as a game with no real intention of buying.

Do I need a receipt for every purchase?

Yes, definitely. The receipt must include the dealer's name and address, phone and e-mail, your name, and a full description of the coin. Don't be surprised if your receipt includes an added amount for sales tax. Full-time dealers are required to include it and, increasingly, state agencies are monitoring compliance. You should expect an equally detailed receipt for purchases you make at a live coin auction.

What recourse do I have if I'm not satisfied with a purchase?

Many dealers will gladly accept merchandise for refund if it's returned in the same condition and within the stated deadline. If a coin you buy sight unseen is in a sealed holder, it must be returned, without having been tampered with, in the same sealed condition. But you always should ask about a dealer's return policy, and a receipt that describes the item is your first line of defense. It's not uncommon for high-grade Mint State coins (63 and higher) to be sold at one grading, but argued to be of a lesser grade when returned or resold to the original dealer.

Online Auctions

Where can I find online auctions?

eBay is the most popular auction site on the Internet. When you call up the home page, at http://www.ebay.com, you'll see that the site is organized by items of interest. Whether you're a buyer or a seller, there are buttons you can click for help and additional information.

The Importance of Eye Appeal

As we've pointed out, coin grading is not an exact science. While there are widely accepted guidelines for determining the grade of a circulated coin, grading Mint State coins—on an eleven-point scale from MS-60 to MS-70—involves a lot of nuance and subjective judgments.

Beyond the tangible issues of nicks, scratches, planchet defects, and other forms of damage (collectively called detractions), there's a set of positive qualities commonly called eye appeal that can make the difference of a point or more in a coin's grade. These include luster, which is the reflective brilliance of the coin (especially in the field areas); toning, which is the natural oxidation of the coin's surface from contact with the atmosphere; and strike, which is the depth and clarity of the minted image. Strike, especially, is determined by the newness of the die. These qualities can make an otherwise respectable coin a standout. While the grade may be unaffected, the seller will recognize that a particular coin is a "killer" or a "rocket" and demand a higher price.

Amazon.com and Yahoo Auctions are two other rapidly growing online auction sites. By visiting a popular search engine such as www.google.com and entering "coin auction" as your search term, you'll generate a long list of other sites to check out, too.

How do I find the coins I'm interested in?

Try searching first under the most common terms you can think of. If you collect complete sets of circulated coinage by year and/or mint mark, you might cast a wide net by starting your search with a year. If you collect by design or denomination, try a more targeted search, such as "Indian Head cent" or "Lincoln cent."

Always remember that sellers are by no means uniformly knowledgeable or precise, so it pays to do variant keyword searches. "Indian Head cent" and "Indian Head penny" will turn up different listings, and the latter will show more offerings from sellers who describe their coins in nontechnical terms, and often overstate rarity or condition. If you have the time to search listings, you can use the auction's categorical layout as a way into the subcategory.

What's the best online-bidding strategy?

Although some people like to open with their highest bid at the start of an auction (to discourage others from bidding), others prefer to wait until the last possible moment before the auction closes to place their bid. That's because bidders must enter their user name, so anyone can use the search engine to track other items a particular bidder is interested in. That way, they may come across items they otherwise might not have found. By waiting until the last moment to bid, you can minimize this method of discovery.

The practice of entering a bid just before the auction closes, called sniping, is considered unfair by some because it may not allow an item to reach its true price potential. But whether you place your maximum bid early or at the last minute, if there are multiple bidders for an item, the highest maximum bid will automatically top all others by the auction's standard increment, even if this occurs in the final seconds before closing. The only difference is that the bidding takes place at the speed of light—faster than any human auctioneer could call the bids! Many new auction sites prevent sniping altogether by extending the deadline for a specified length of time if a bid comes in at the last minute.

What are seller's reserve prices?

The reserve is the lowest price that a seller is willing to accept. This amount usually isn't disclosed until the close of the auction. If the item reaches its reserve price, the auction site will indicate that the reserve is met and the item will be sold.

How does the transaction take place if I make a winning bid?

If you've placed the winning bid, you'll see your user name listed on the item's auction page. The auction site then will notify both you and the seller and provide your respective e-mail addresses.

The seller should send the successful bidder a note explaining shipping and payment options. Once you've made payment and received the item, it's customary to notify the seller that it was received in good condition.

What if my coin arrives and it isn't what was described?

The seller should let you return it and should refund your money. But if the coin was accurately described and you're simply unhappy with it, you're

A Bit of History within Reach: The Indian Head Cent, 1859–1909

The coveted Indian Head cent is so called because the obverse depicts Liberty wearing a feathered headdress. Mint designer and engraver James B. Longacre (a tiny sideways L is tucked at the nape of Liberty's neck, easily visible on MS- and AU-grade coins), is reputed to have used his daughter as his model for Liberty. In ads for these coins, you'll often see four diamonds mentioned: these are located in Liberty's headband but wear off quickly in circulated examples. Even a weakly struck Uncirculated coin may not show all four of the diamonds.

The Indian Head cent was the second issue in the era of Small Cents, as distinguished from the Large Cents that preceded them (a Flying Eagle Small Cent was minted from 1857 to 1858). Truth be told, the value of the copper required to mint a Large Cent had become greater than the face value. Thus the U.S. Treasury was actually losing money by making them!

The Indian Head cent is available in many years and mint marks for under $100 in EF-40 grade.

A 1901 Indian Head cent.
Photos courtesy of Rare Coin Galleries of Seattle, Inc.

probably stuck. Be sure to read the sellers' return policies posted with each listing. If you're not satisfied with what you read there, e-mail the seller to obtain the assurance you're looking for. If it's not offered, move on to another auction.

When the transaction is complete, each party should "post feedback" into the other party's profile. If the seller described the item accurately, shipped it promptly, packaged it sufficiently, and worked to resolve any disputes, then it's customary to give positive feedback. Negative feedback should be a last resort, reserved for instances in which all efforts to resolve a dispute have failed.

What are the pros and cons of buying in an online auction?

Many coin collectors are thrilled to have access to thousands of coins, but some are justifiably nervous about doing business in cyberspace. Secure credit-card payment services, such as PayPal and BillPoint, are helping to allay concerns about sending payment to a stranger before the item is even shipped. But at some point, payment is released, and you take possession of the item. If you're unhappy with it later on, you may have limited recourse.

The majority of coins sold in online auctions are not slabbed and graded by a recognized service. You're trusting a digital photo or scan of a photo that may not be well lighted, accurate for color, or in sharp focus. Even with a superb photo, you can't examine the coin as closely as you could in person using a 5X or 10X magnifying loupe. If you're unsure about bidding—especially on a high-ticket item—don't hesitate to inquire in great detail about the coin's condition, or to request additional photos. And always get a guarantee that you'll be able to return the piece for a refund if it's not in the condition advertised. Save all e-mail from the seller with regard to condition, terms, and returns.

Live Auctions

How do I find coin auctions?

Auctions that take place before a live audience range from club show events, attended primarily by dealers and collectors, to large auctions in urban centers where museums, coin galleries, collectors and their proxies, and interested parties from around the world may converge. Numismatic hobby publications and their Web sites list these auctions, both major and minor.

What's the role of the auctioneer?

The auctioneer is the agent for the auction inventory's owners who actually takes bids for the "lots," whether individual items or groups of items. He or she will announce each lot to be sold and briefly describe it. A slide projector is often used to show an enlarged image of the coin on a wall or screen. Auctioneers usually are paid a commission based on final selling price, so it's to their advantage to get the highest bids.

How can I prepare for an auction?

The most important thing is to inspect any coins you're interested in first-hand, before the auction begins. Many auctions schedule preview periods, sometimes the day before or early on the morning of the auction. Do not bid on a coin you haven't examined carefully.

Decide beforehand what you're willing to bid. This will help you avoid being carried away in a frenzied bidding war and paying more than the coin is worth. In arriving at your maximum price, be sure to factor in state sales tax and any buyer's premium (the auction's commission charged to the winning bidder) that may apply.

Is it difficult to register so I can bid?

Not at all. You probably can even do it by mail. If you have a driver's license and a credit card, you're all set. Some auctions also ask for credit references and a bank reference if you plan to pay by check. You'll be assigned a bidder number, and at the more established auctions you'll be issued a paddle showing your number.

Exactly how does the bidding work?

As with online auctions, some items may have reserve prices. The auctioneer will determine the opening bid based on this reserve and on any absentee bids received before the sale. Often, bidding starts at about half to two-thirds of the item's "low estimate." For example, if a coin is expected to sell between $600 and $1,000, the auctioneer may start the bidding at $300 or $400.

Then, as bids come in, the bid price will escalate—usually in increments corresponding to the amount. For instance, between $100 and $500, the bid may increase in increments of $10; when the bidding reaches $500, it may increase in increments of $25. Once the bidding has topped out and the auctioneer receives no further bids, he'll close, usually with the words "Fair warning; going once; going twice; sold." If you happen to be the successful bidder, you show your paddle or call out your bid number. In the event that the bidding doesn't reach the reserve price, the auctioneer simply pulls the item and it's not sold (this is called a pass). Auctioneers sometimes cover unsold items by announcing that the item was "bought in," or "sold to the house," or some other term that sounds more like a sale than a no-sale. Auction houses' reputations are thus maintained by the perception that they effectively sell every lot that passes through their hands.

Experienced collectors will tell you to avoid making the first bid. But once bidding is under way, make sure the auctioneer can see you. Don't hold off until the end or otherwise try to "time" your bids. Just speak clearly, make eye contact with the auctioneer, bid until you're done, and then stop. Good luck!

Can I still bid if I can't be present at the auction?

Yes. Of course, it's always best to bid in person. But if you can't be there, preregister and submit bids for all coins you're interested in. Once the auction is under way, your bid will be executed as if you were there.

An even better strategy is to bid by phone. Phone bidding lets you participate live in the auction. However, you should still set your maximums and go no further by phone than you would have in person. Established auction houses have several phone lines manned by staff who will call you when your desired lot comes up and then stay on the line during the bidding, to increase your bid as instructed. There's no additional commission charge for executing phone bids.

Another option is to arrange for a trusted fellow collector or dealer to act as your proxy at the auction. Again, pre-set your maximums. Our experts recommend either phone or proxy bidding instead of absentee bidding, for the following reason: If the auctioneer is holding an absentee bid that's considerably over the low estimate, he may decide to start the bidding higher than he would have otherwise. So, even if your absentee bid wins, you may end up paying more than you would have if you'd been bidding by phone or proxy. If you use a proxy—who can also be your expert in examining the coins for eye appeal—be prepared to pay him a 5 percent commission on the winning prices.

How do I claim my winnings?

You may pick up your coins at the auction house following the auction or, in some cases, have them shipped to you. And remember, once the gavel drops and you've won an item, legal title transfers to you. Any damage or loss beyond that point is your responsibility.

Don't even think of not honoring your winning bid. When you bid, you enter into a legal contract to purchase at the agreed price, and you'll be held to your agreement.

What are the pros and cons of buying at live auctions?

In today's market, some of the very best coins are sold by auction houses. But competition can be fierce, as evidenced by the astronomical prices sometimes realized. Yet, just as every auction has items that sell for far too much, every auction also has its share of outright bargains.

As a beginning collector, you may enjoy the electricity of a live auction, especially an important one conducted by a prestige house. But it's best to watch the sparks fly from a safe distance until you have more experience. If you really feel the need to stretch your wings at an auction, start with a reputable local or regional auction—perhaps one held in conjunction with a coin show—before you plunge into the big league. For the most part, rare and high-grade coins dominate and the prices are substantial. Proof sets and singles may also be offered: if they pass your close, in-person inspection, this may be a safer place for your initial foray into bidding.

COLLECTOR'S COMPASS

Win or lose, one of the benefits of following, attending, or bidding in a major auction is having the catalog as a record of the event. If you attend in person, mark down the prices realized for every lot that holds even slight interest for you. (If you purchase the catalog, the auction will commonly send you a list of all prices realized, but sometimes only upon request.) Increasingly, the big houses post their results on their Web sites, too. These records serve as useful reference points to current values paid in competitive situations. They'll be good reminders, or even bargaining points, when you see a comparable coin in a shop or an online auction. The very same coins may show up in the marketplace again soon; the catalog will help you recognize them and remember what was paid for them.

The Walking Liberty half-dollar, issued 1916–47, is appreciated especially for the design of the eagle on the reverse. This example was struck in 1938. *Photos courtesy of Rare Coin Galleries of Seattle, Inc.*

NOW THAT YOU'RE READY TO START COLLECTING

The Collector's Toolbox

You won't need a lot of fancy tools, but there are a few essential aids that will help you make judgments about condition, authenticity, and, in some cases, mint errors.

Magnifying Loupe

The single most essential tool for a new collector to acquire and learn to use is a good-quality loupe. While you can examine coins reasonably well with the naked eye, mint marks, design details, and wear are easier to read with a magnifier.

Any examination to confirm that a graded coin is what it's claimed to be, or to do an informal grading yourself, must take into account all evidence of wear and detractions, as well as the qualities of the strike itself.

The Hastings Triplet loupe (10X) made by Bausch & Lomb is recommended by many numismatic experts. If you want to keep your initial cost down, a plastic-framed 5X-to-7X lens is sufficient. Higher-power magnifiers (over 10X) limit the area of the coin you can see at one time, and we don't recommend them as the only magnifying tool you'll ever need.

Bausch & Lomb
5x magnifier

Light Source

A concentrated light source under which you can tip a coin from side to side to cast light obliquely over its surface is the only effective way to reveal flaws and wear. It may be helpful to have a flashlight, but you need one hand to hold the coin and the other to hold your loupe. So, a stationary light source is preferable. Most shops—and many dealers at shows—will have an incandescent or high-intensity light available for customers.

Avoid using sunlight or overhead lighting, especially fluorescent bulbs, to examine coins.

Gloves and Soft Fabric or Pad

Cheap, soft cotton gloves are useful for handling coins to avoid damaging the surface with skin oil or leaving fingerprints. Thin latex gloves are also acceptable, though some find them uncomfortable to wear for more than a few minutes.

Dealers may provide a cushion or pad, but it's smart to bring your own. A coin dropped on a hard surface—or onto another coin—can be damaged. Check jewelry supply houses for pads and trays; you'll want one or more for your own use at home.

Coin Holders

You'll do well to bring immediate protection for raw coins you may acquire. The Mylar plastic pockets known as flips are a convenient way to carry coins home. Or you may opt for cardboard-and-Mylar window holders, called 2 X 2s, for their size (2" X 2"), which require a pocket stapler to fasten. Most dealers in shops or at shows will package your coins for you in one of these kinds of holders, but it pays to be prepared for the unprepared.

COLLECTOR'S COMPASS ™

Coin holders made with polyvinyl chloride (PVC) are the bane of coin collectors. Pliable PVC holders, most commonly found as flips, can destroy the value of your coins. Over time—and with the right combination of temperature and humidity—the PVC will liquefy into a greenish goo that will forever deface your valued coins. Buy your holders from trusted sources, make sure they do not contain PVC, and make a habit of transferring any unslabbed coins you buy at a show from the dealers' holders to ones you know to be safe as soon as you can.

Pocket Stapler and Staple Puller

Most dealers who sell even lower-grade coins will encase them in flips or 2 X 2s. If you're seriously interested in a coin, it's not impolite to ask to have it removed from its container. Either the seller or you should remove all staples from the holder first to avoid any chance of scratching the coin.

Notepad and Pencil or Pen

Even if you've preprinted a "want list" of particular coins you're seeking, you may still need to make notes. Especially at a show, you may need to note addresses of dealers or other collectors who mention something they may be willing to sell.

Secure Pack or Bag

A large tote is necessary only if you're interested in buying books, coin folders, or albums. But a secure way to carry coins is something to plan for. Zippered fanny or waist packs work well; so do zippered shoulder bags with multiple compartments. Depending on the season, you may opt for a vest with zippered pockets as a way to keep your treasures "close to your heart."

Some coin experts advise you not to carry any kind of bag at coin shows or numismatic conventions. They also counsel that you remove your show badge outside the convention area. Coin shows can attract savvy thieves and pickpockets, and wearing a show badge or carrying a bag is an advertisement that you're likely to be carrying money that's worth a lot more than its face value.

Black Light

A black light is not recommended for beginners, but you should know that alterations to coins, such as scratches or nicks that have been filled with epoxy mixed with fine metal shavings, can be revealed under black light.

Price Guide

You should also have the current edition of the Whitman Red Book, formally titled *The Official Red Book: A Guide Book of United States Coins,* by R. S. Yeoman and edited by Kenneth Bressett, published by St. Martin's Press annually. It is the most widely recognized source of information for all U.S. coins. Values for multiple grades are given for most.

The Most Popular U.S. Coin to Collect: The Lincoln Cent

Uncirculated 1909 Lincoln Wheat Ears cent. Until 1909, no actual person's portrait had ever appeared on a regular-circulation U.S. coin. This example shows how a fingerprint can be permanently "etched" into the surface of a copper-alloy coin. *Photos courtesy of Rare Coin Galleries of Seattle, Inc.*

Perhaps not surprisingly, informal surveys estimate that 95 percent of U.S. coin collectors gather the Lincoln cent. It was the first U.S. circulating coin to picture an actual person, after more than a century of allegorical depictions of Liberty, and has remained in circulation longer than any other U.S. coin. In its first year of issue, 1909 (the centennial year of Lincoln's birth), five different circulating versions were minted (including the "S over horizontal S" mint-mark anomaly). Double-die varieties were made in 1917 and 1936. In 1943, the cents were struck in zinc-coated steel due to the wartime shortage of copper, but a handful of copper planchets found their way into the presses, creating yet another object of quest for coin collectors (caution: counterfeits of this mint error abound). From 1944 to 1946, surplus cartridge cases were melted for the minting of cents, giving these coins a slightly different hue.

The original "wheat ears" reverse design was changed in 1959 to a depiction of the Lincoln Memorial, in observance of the 150th anniversary of Lincoln's birth. It's a safe bet that the coin will undergo a second facelift come the bicentennial observance in 2009.

The best news is that this coin is affordable: the 2001 edition of the Red Book lists only three coins in the entire series over $100 in Extremely Fine circulated condition, and most can be had for under $10 each.

What Determines the Value of Coins?

First, review "Understanding the Perplexing Business of Coin Grading" on pages 36–38 to refresh your memory of the letter-number designations used to grade circulated and uncirculated coins. Then this discussion of factors that impact values will begin to make sense as you examine coins at shops and shows. You'll find there's no substitute for studying graded coins closely in person.

Condition: High Impact on Value

Coins are found in the marketplace in every condition, from Mint State to heavily worn and damaged—including coins that may have been drilled, filed, or otherwise defaced (commonly called culls). Numismatic experts advise that—except for rarities and eighteenth-century coins—coins graded Poor are not worth collecting; even coins graded Good are so heavily worn that they hold little appeal for collectors. For newcomers who want to collect graded coins, the Very Good (VG-8) designation is a good starting level.

Coin grading is undeniably technical in nature. *The Official A.N.A. Grading Standards for United States Coins,* fifth edition (1996), is the best single reference for a beginner trying to grasp the nuances of coin grades. But beyond the technical grading of a coin's state of preservation, other "market grading" criteria have been introduced by third-party grading services. In addition to indicators of wear and detractions that may determine a coin's technical grade—assessed by the ANA's standards through its grading service, ANACS, starting in 1979—the competing grading services also evaluated the quality of strike, luster, toning, and the overall "beauty" of a coin. This difference in approach led the ANA to divest ANACS by selling it to Amos Press in 1990. The current-day ANACS uses a market grading approach and is among the top third-party grading services used by U.S. coin collectors.

Today, the professional grading services—as well as numismatic experts—continue to debate the subtleties of grading. Most of the attention is at the level of Almost Uncirculated, Uncirculated, and Mint State coins, where a difference of one point can impact value by thousands of dollars. Here are the most critical elements in evaluating condition—that is, preservation.

Wear and Damage

While technically not a U.S. coin, since the Kingdom of Hawaii was not annexed until 1898 and made a U.S. Territory in 1900, this 1847 Hawaiian cent comes, literally, from now-American soil. The corrosion resulted from the coin's being buried in a field as insurance for a bountiful crop, a common practice of the time. *Photo courtesy of Rare Coin Galleries of Seattle, Inc.*

- Normal usage wear. Circulated coins begin to acquire damage from the time they leave the die-stamping press and tumble into boxes or bags with other newly minted coins. Once they leave the banking system, they pass from hand to hand, are shuffled in coin drawers, jingle in change purses and pockets, pass through vending machines—and the occasional washer and dryer—where they suffer abrasions that gradually wear down their surfaces.

- Unusual usage wear. You'll see coins with holes drilled in them, faces filed down, or bent from being used as screwdrivers. Others may be stained or corroded from environmental factors, such as salt water or chemicals. You may come across coins that were used as jewelry—pendants, bracelets, brooches, and the like.

- Grease, oil, and dirt. Circulating coins gather fingerprints from skin oils, and collect lint and dirt in crevices, around their rims, and in the reeding on their edges.

- Acid stains and corrosion. Tiny droplets of saliva on the surface of a silver coin will, over time, cause spotting and discoloration. Coins that have been dipped in a mild acid cleaning solution lose a microscopic layer of their toning, or patina, as well as possibly some of the metal itself. Coins stored in contact with a polyvinyl chloride (PVC) holder can take on a gummy, greenish coating. Sulfite chemicals in paper can discolor copper and silver coins stored in paper envelopes.

- Environmental damage. This can include stains from moisture and air pollutants. Molds and bacteria can cause detractions if allowed to collect on coin surfaces. Humidity and atmospheric gases—including cigarette and other kinds of smoke—will affect the toning of silver and copper coins. All silver coins gradually darken if left undisturbed. Some darken evenly and with interesting color variations. Others may become spotty and unattractive due to fingerprints, acid droplets, or exposure to humidity and airborne pollutants. Gold coins are much less reactive and retain most of their original luster—even when exposed to salt water. Copper coins are the most susceptible to darkening and discoloring. Prolonged exposure to sunlight will gradually dull the luster of silver and copper coins. Being buried in the earth or spending time under water will similarly affect a coin's surfaces.

- Cracks, scratches, and dents. Depressions, pits, and cracks in coins are usually caused by imperfections in the planchet from which the coin was struck. Scratches, dents, dings, and gouges begin at the mint (these are called bag or contact marks) and continue throughout the circulating life of the coin.

Alterations

Mint marks have been removed, added, or altered on coins. Dates have been changed. Deep nicks have been filled with epoxy mixed with fine metal shavings. The obverse of one coin and the reverse of another may be filed smooth and bonded together to create a "single" coin. These alterations, and others, result in fake coins of questionable value. It should be noted, however, that sometimes coins are defaced not to deceive but as a form of artistic expression, and these "coins" may become collectible (see "Love Tokens, Hobo Nickels, and Other Fates That Befell Coins" on page 84)—but almost never by serious numismatists.

Repairs, Restoration, and Cleaning

Cleaning is a so-called improvement that's generally frowned upon by serious collectors. Polishing coins with abrasive brushes, called "whizzing," may appear to the untrained eye to enhance luster. But under a loupe, the whizzed surface has a granular appearance that's nothing like the way the coin left the mint. These practices seriously detract from value.

Original Packaging

Packaging is significant for proof sets and coins graded by professional services. Proofs retain their value in their original sealed holder (though a modern proof coin that's been "cracked out" of its holder, but is otherwise uncompromised, may be graded as being in the same state as one in the holder). Grading services use their own sonically sealed packages; nowadays, they often feature

An example from 1875 (with added chop mark) of the Trade silver dollar, authorized by Congress in 1873 for use by American merchants in Asia. Congress revoked the Trade dollar's legal tender status in the United States in 1876. *Photos courtesy of Rare Coin Galleries of Seattle, Inc.*

Love Tokens, Hobo Nickels, and
Other Fates That Befell Coins

Throughout American history, U.S. coins have provided "canvases" for the creative efforts of intrepid and would-be engravers. The apex of this practice followed the Civil War, when love tokens became a fad. A coin was filed or planed smooth on one or both sides, then an original design was engraved by hand. The only requirement was to start with a U.S. coin in circulation—usually a cent or half-cent, sometimes a dime or quarter. Rarely were larger-denomination pieces like silver dollars so treated. In the late nineteenth century, for many workers a dollar represented an entire week's wages.

Coins were engraved with initials, sentiments of love and devotion, dedications for special occasions, or pictorial designs. Some were naïve, even crude. Others were complex and sophisticated. They could be holed, enclosed in a bezel to be worn as a pendant, soldered to a hanging loop or backpin to wear as a brooch, or made into a stickpin. Today, there are more than two hundred members of the Love Token Society.

During the Depression years following 1929, the Buffalo nickel was a popular subject for itinerant "artists," who reworked the Indian's portrait on the obverse into a wide assortment of faces and caricatures. These so-called Hobo Nickels are avidly collected by a small, but passionate, group. *Photo courtesy of Rare Coin Galleries of Seattle, Inc.*

A comparable twentieth-century expression of coin altering took root soon after the Buffalo Nickel five-cent piece made its appearance in 1913. Itinerant hobos took to carving variations on the obverse portrait image. Many were modeled after their friends; some depicted fishing, firefighting, or other occupations. Some "artists" attacked the bison on the reverse, turning him into a donkey or elephant (especially popular for sale to Republicans and Democrats, respectively), or some other animal.

As with other forms of hobo art, the artists bartered for meals with their work or sold it for gain. Today, there's a lively market for hobo art of all kinds, and there are still some practitioners at work. Is it any surprise that there's an Original Hobo Nickel Society?

Another novel form of coin destruction got its start at the 1893 Columbian International Exposition in Chicago. There, you could have a perfectly good cent passed between two heavy rollers that squashed it into a thin, elongated strip and embossed the name of the fair. Elongated cents became immensely popular as souvenirs of amusement parks, arcades, fairs, boardwalks, and the like in the early decades of the twentieth century. In recent years, the fad has taken off again—to the point that collectors can't keep up with the output and have to specialize. If this area strikes your fancy, you're moving beyond the bounds of coin collecting into exonumia, but you can join like-minded souls in the Elongated Collectors club.

Visit http://localsonly.wilmington.net/mwallace to view "Numismatic Americana," part of a Web site maintained by Mike Wallace, for more information on all of these subjects, contact information for joining the clubs and societies mentioned, and introductions to a range of other fascinating areas.

holograms to make them tamperproof. As long as these packages are sealed and untampered with, numismatists and experienced collectors accept the validity and authenticity of the original grade as established by the service.

Otherwise, circulating coins are rarely, if ever, individually packaged at the mint or thereafter.

Intrinsic Characteristics: High Impact on Value

Mint State coins especially are often described in rapturous adjectives similar to those used to describe fine wine. The intrinsic characteristics that most often receive attention from collectors are detailed here.

Luster. The brilliant reflective surface finish of an unused coin carries its own appeal. Gold coins retain luster, while silver and copper coins lose theirs as they age. You'll find the term "blast white" used—especially with silver dollars—to describe a high-luster coin.

Toning. The effects of metal reacting with the environment are variable, and describing them is highly subjective. Silver coins may tone evenly, taking on a rich overall patina, or they may acquire multicolored patterns—radiating bands, concentric circles, or rainbow effects—that some collectors find attractive. Copper coins darken relatively quickly, but they may variably acquire ruddy, deep reds or even chocolate hues. Coins may be artificially toned in an attempt to enhance their appearance.

Strike. Dies wear out, so coins struck early in the die's life span will produce clearer, cleaner outlines and details. Similarly, the pressure of the strike can vary, resulting in deeper relief and more minute details, or shallow relief and loss of detail. An especially perfect strike may earn the description Deep Mirror Proof-Like (DMPL), most often applied to exceptional Mint State silver dollars. Finally, some collections emphasize minute differences among coins struck from different dies. With multiple mint branches using sometimes thousands of dies made in the Philadelphia mint from multiple hubs, variations are myriad over the course of a coin's years of mintage.

Eye appeal. When all the technical elements of condition, plus these three intrinsic qualities, are combined in an outstanding example of the designer's and engraver's art, the result is a coin of almost ineffable beauty and appeal to numismatic enthusiasts. In these cases, the grade is only a baseline for the ultimate value that a collector may place on the coin.

Unusual design. Certain designs go in and out of favor. The Double Eagle ($20) gold piece designed by Saint-Gaudens was minted in its original form only during part of the year 1907. Known among collectors as the High Relief Double Eagle, this coin possesses a sculptural quality. Only 11,250 pieces were struck. Treasury officials quickly realized the coins' impracticality, as the height of relief made stacking it difficult and contributed to excessive and accelerated wear. The coins minted later in 1907 and through 1933 used a much shallower version of the design, with a much stronger rim. A High Relief 1907 Saint-Gaudens Double Eagle graded MS-60 carries a 2001 Red Book value of $7,250.

Unusual detail. The details of folds in Liberty's drapery, curls in her hair, or the feathers in an eagle's tail may be appreciated by collectors, but they don't necessarily make one type of coin more desirable than another.

Unusual details within a type of coin's minting, as dies may have changed subtly over the years, are of interest and do have bearing on value. Likewise, the amount of detail may be an indication of a superior strike in an uncirculated coin and may help a circulated coin achieve a higher grade as a measure of preservation.

Production errors. There's enormous collector interest in the mistakes the Mint has made over the years. Recently, it's the notorious "Sac Mule." This misstrike resulted from the mating of

Off-center Jefferson nickel. *Photos courtesy of Rare Coin Galleries of Seattle, Inc.*

a Washington twenty-five-cent obverse die with the Sacagawea-dollar reverse die. While only a handful of these misstrikes made it into circulation, they were quickly recognized by the numismatic community and have brought prices in excess of $40,000 at auction. However, not all mint errors bring such high prices. A three-legged error version of the Buffalo five-cent piece was struck at the Denver mint in 1937 when a rushed die repair inadvertently polished off the right front leg. An authentic example of this error is priced in the 2001 Red Book at $450 in EF-40 grade; an MS-63 example is listed at $3,200. Because the error consists of a missing detail, enterprising counterfeiters have responded by trying to convincingly remove the right front legs from normal 1937D five-cent pieces, which the Red Book values at only $2 in the same EF-40 grade and $20 in MS-63!

Design variations. Numismatists make fine distinctions about variations in the design of a particular type of coin. For instance, some examples of the Indian Head cent show the lowermost feather of the figure's headdress pointing to different letters in the word "America." Some years of minting may include a large-date version as well as a small-date version, or variations in the size, weight, or placement of a mint mark. Such variations result from different dies being used at the various mint branches, or from the evolution of designs used over a period of years. Some have significant impact on the value of individual coins.

Age: Low Impact on Value

Determining the age of U.S. coins is a straightforward matter. Since the minting of the Fugio (or Franklin) cents in 1787, coins have carried the year of minting as part of their design. Starting in 1838 with the establishment of branches in Dahlonega (Georgia), Charlotte (North Carolina), and New Orleans, mint marks were added to the date to record the place of minting (coins minted in Philadelphia carried no mint mark prior to 1942–45, and following that period were again blank until 1979).

The age of a coin is not a high determinant of its value. The number of coins minted, the population of surviving examples, and the state of preservation of those survivors are much more

Off-center 1900 Indian Head cent. Note the broken collar on the obverse. *Photos courtesy of Rare Coin Galleries of Seattle, Inc.*

significant to value. The interest level among collectors for a particular type of coin at any given time is also more important to value than age.

Rarity and Demand: High Impact on Value

Rarity and demand—along with state of preservation—are the primary axes in determining values. The U.S. Mint has kept detailed and accurate records of the number of each type of coin minted, at each of its branches, for each year, and for most changes of design. Thus, the relative rarity of coins in terms of the total number minted is well known.

Since the advent of professional grading services in the late 1970s, accounts have been kept of the surviving population for each coin design, year, and mint mark, in an attempt to provide a refined measure of rarity. The drawback to this record is that there is no limit to the number of times the same coin may be submitted to the same or different services for grading. Thus, surviving-population numbers are prone to inflation.

Mint errors and misstrikes, in which a coin may have been either struck more than once, with slightly overlapping impressions, or partially struck, with part of the blank planchet still showing, constitute their own categories of rarities.

Anomalies are generally highly valued and receive a lot of attention in the numismatic press soon after they are discovered. Their rarity is tracked as individual examples come to light. Sometimes these mistakes enter circulation through human error, failed quality control, or deliberate intention. However, once the newsworthiness of these errors wears thin, the fascination with them also often wanes, and initial white-hot values may plummet. Which brings us to the ultimate reality of coin values: A coin may be in a wonderful state of preservation; it may be a member of a small population of coins of its type, a bona fide rarity. But if demand for a coin is not greater than its availability, the value may remain modest. Condition and rarity—individually or even together—are not enough to give a coin astronomical value. Demand can.

Attribution: Low Impact on Value

In the late nineteenth century and throughout the twentieth, it increasingly became the practice for designers and engravers to include a minute monogram or initial somewhere in their designs. In these cases, the names, the mark used, and its location are all highly documented.

For instance, George T. Morgan's initial *M* appears on Liberty Head dollars minted between 1878 and 1921; they are called Morgan dollars. Designs similarly named for their designer are the Barber dime and Barber quarter. Charles E. Barber was chief engraver of the Mint for several years and designed fifty-cent pieces in addition to the coins mentioned. Most coins are collected by type rather than by designer, so even the premier names have low impact on coin values.

Provenance: Variable Impact on Value

Major collections go on the market with regularity, usually at high-profile auctions. Visit the Bowers and Merena Web site (see "Resources to Further Your Collecting" on page 112) to get a taste of the sums realized when world-class collections are sold. While it's difficult to predict or to generalize the premium value that a coin can command with a name like Pittman, Garrett, Norweb, Childs, Bass, or Eliasberg attached to it, there's no question that once a coin leaves the cabinet of a great collector, it remains connected with its former owner's name.

Judging Authenticity

There are basically three kinds of less-than-authentic coins found in circulation and in the coin marketplace.

1. Altered coins have had an element added, removed, or changed. A mint mark or other detail may have been planed or filed off. A mint mark or engraver's initials may have been added, or a date changed. These kinds of alterations are intended to make less valuable coins appear more valuable in an attempt to deceive.

2. Cast counterfeits are made from molds that use authentic minted coins as the masters. These fakes are meant to pass for real money, rather than deceive scrutinizing numismatists. Cast counterfeits are fairly easy to spot as second-generation coins—their relief may be soft, the fields and devices granular.

3. Die-struck counterfeits are the most difficult to detect, even for professionals. They have been created by engravers as copies of authentic coins and struck using techniques similar to those used by the U.S. Mint. Sometimes it is only an expert's sensitivity to an extremely subtle and minute variation from authentic examples that allows him to pick out the fake. Such sensitivity is the product of a great deal of specialized study and examination of many, many coins. Counterfeiters' arrogance—or pride in their work, depending on your perspective—is sometimes satisfied by deliberately leaving behind a trace of their fakery. The 1907 High Relief

Saint-Gaudens Double Eagle has been counterfeited in a die-struck version that carries a tiny Greek letter omega inside the eagle's claw on the reverse. The omega is a dead giveaway that the coin is a counterfeit, but otherwise a very convincing one.

As a beginner, you're not likely to be considering the coins that are most frequently altered or counterfeited, because they tend to be at the high end of the value spectrum. Nevertheless, get in the habit of examining coins closely, with special attention to areas that are frequently subject to alteration. Several books on counterfeits and altered coins provide guidance, many showing altered areas in extreme close-up. If your specialty includes coins that are known to be counterfeited or altered, it's worth your while to study this literature. You may come upon a dealer who keeps a few counterfeit coins in his shop as a way of testing collectors or as instructional pieces. There's usually a sadder-but-wiser lament that goes along with the lesson, whereby the dealer recounts how he was burned by someone who passed the coin off as authentic.

If you get serious about studying counterfeits, contact the ANA about attending one of its counterfeit-detection seminars, often given in an abbreviated version at the national convention, and in full week-long form at the summer session held in Colorado Springs each July. U.S. Treasury officers participate as faculty along with professional numismatists, and the sessions are open to beginners.

The Business of Collecting

Maintaining Good Records

There are some keys to building and protecting your collection that will pay dividends and help you enjoy the hobby. Unless you amass a huge and extremely valuable collection, record keeping won't take much of your time.

First—and foremost—save your receipts! It's a good idea to staple the dealer's business card to each receipt. For online transactions, save copies of all e-mail between you and the seller. Keeping track of the people you have bought from is helpful for many reasons:

- You may need to contact the dealer because of a problem or question about a coin you've purchased. When buying in person, your purchases are likely nonreturnable; the exception is a coin that turns out to be inauthentic. But most mail-order and online coin sellers offer a limited-time return privilege.

- You may want to sell back or trade up with the same dealer. As you develop productive relationships with reputable dealers, it's likely that they'll watch out for upgrade coins in your collecting interests. Some or even all of the value of your current example may be credited against the purchase of a better coin.

- You may want the dealer to look for particular items. While many dealers are too busy or disinclined to follow up reliably, you may be pleasantly surprised to get a phone call or e-mail long after leaving your want list with a dealer in a shop or at a show.

- You may want to compare the dealer's original asking price with what you actually paid. Coin dealers generally operate on a smaller margin (10 to 20 percent) than in many antiques-and-collectible categories. Thus, there's usually a relatively narrow range of prices for accurately graded coins among reputable dealers. However, there are dealers who consistently price to allow for discounting, and having a record of that practice will help you in future transactions with them.

Keeping an Inventory

Maintain a record of each addition to your collection, including date and place of purchase, condition, price, and seller, along with any details important to you. There are a number of software programs designed for inventory management that will simplify this task.

Photographic records of your coins are a must. Videos are inadequate to show the details and qualities of individual coins, so they won't be of much use in presenting a coin for sale, in legal matters, or in making an insurance claim. If you're capable of taking focused, close-up color photographs (avoiding areas of glare, hot spots, and other deficiencies), make photo prints of your valuable

Creating a Want List

Your want list is essentially your personal advertisement as a collector. Therefore, it requires careful consideration, and our experts, who spend most of their time on the other side of the counter, have shared what they most appreciate in a want list.

- Perhaps obviously, your contact information should be clearly presented, with options in order of preference—for example: name, home phone, business phone, and e-mail. Mailing address, if given, should be a post-office box. Registered, insured, first-class mail is still the most secure form of shipment for coins, and you don't need to advertise where you live to use it.

- List the items that you're seeking as specifically as possible, and limit the number of items on any list to five or six entries. This accomplishes two objectives: (1) it's more likely that the recipient will hold your wants in his memory; and (2) it projects the message that you are a focused, serious collector—especially if the dealer specializes in the items on your list. If your wants are extensive, make up a few different lists rather than one long one.

- Don't list series (e.g., Mercury dimes, 1916–45, all mint marks); rather, specify the individual coins you are seeking. At the other extreme, don't

coins and store them along with your other records. If you have similar skills with a digital camera and your home computer is equipped with a CD burner, you can make photo CDs. Consider having a professional photographer do this work if you can't achieve sharp results.

Keep your records in a safe, fireproof location in your home, and a second set in a safe-deposit box in a separate location. Indeed, if you begin to acquire coins of significant value, a safe-deposit box becomes almost a necessity.

Getting an Appraisal

An appraisal is an expert opinion of the value of a particular coin or coins. It should include a complete description, along with any list an outrageously rare or valuable coin. A knowledgeable collector will speak personally to a dealer he has reason to expect can deliver a highly desirable piece.

- Resist the temptation to wallpaper a coin show with your list or do a shotgun mailing to every dealer on the ANA-certified list. The professional coin-dealer world is a loose network—people know each other, each other's specialties, and do a lot of dealer-to-dealer business to satisfy their clients' needs. Once dealers start querying each other and it becomes evident that you've sent everyone the same list, their attentions are likely to turn to more fruitful prospects.

- It's best to be selective. Talk to a dealer first—by e-mail, phone, or in person—and get a sense that he may be a good source for what you collect before sharing your want list with him. Select primary dealers in different regions to be your extra set of eyes. If you are based on the East Coast, it's a plus for a West Coast dealer to know that you've chosen him to work with in that market.

- Whether you collect casually or aggressively, keep your want list up to date. Few things can be more frustrating to a diligent dealer than to work a collector's want list only to find he's already gotten the coin.

original receipts and descriptions provided by sellers. It must describe condition in detail. Notes on any additional factors that affect value, such as rarity, must be included. Current and anticipated market conditions for the sale of the item should be stated. An estimate of the item's current market value is essential. You must specify at the outset the purpose for having an appraisal done—estate planning, divorce, insurance, donation, etc.—as it will affect the determination of value. National and international associations of certified professional appraisers—such as the International Society of Appraisers (ISA) and the American Appraisers' Association (ASA) list coin experts in their member rosters. If you need an appraisal, engage the services of one of these accredited or certified appraisers.

Be aware that a professional appraisal is an expensive proposition; unless you own coins of considerable value, its cost may exceed the value of your holdings. If you simply want to verify the value of a few coins, you can request a professional verbal opinion from one or more coin dealers whose knowledge you trust. You may have to pay for this service, but it's likely to be much less expensive than having a full appraisal. If the value estimated in the verbal opinion is substantial, by all means proceed with a full appraisal.

An indirect method for establishing the market price of a coin that you think may be valuable is to send it to a professional grading service. Keep in mind, though, that grading services do not place a price or appraised value on a coin.

Today, the primary grading services (see "Resources to Further Your Collecting" on pages 118-119) use a documented method that includes having multiple staff numismatists examine the coin, after which a grading is assigned. The coin is then encapsulated in a plastic holder, along with the details of the coin's type and the grade. The grading services use proprietary packaging and marking.

It's unlikely that you'll need a grading service in your early collecting. If you do, arrange the transaction through your preferred professional coin dealer, as most of the services work through a retail network.

Silver dollar commemorating the 1996 Centennial Olympics (Gymnastics). *Photo courtesy of the U.S. Mint.*

If you're a casual coin collector, you'll likely maintain an awareness of the value and rate of appreciation of your coins by simply following the Red Book from edition to edition and by talking with dealers and other collectors at shows. More ardent collectors may use a magazine's value guide—such as that of *Coin World,* which is updated every three weeks for subscribers. Many collectors monitor the results of online auctions to track current sale prices. If you're willing to pay the price of the subscription, the Greysheet is a weekly publication that many dealers use as the most up-to-date wholesale pricing reference (see "Resources to Further Your Collecting" on pages 113–114).

Insuring Your Collection

Depending on how quickly your collection grows and the value of individual coins in it, you'll probably need more than ordinary homeowner's or renter's insurance before long. Consult your insurance agent to determine the extent of your coverage, if any, under "ordinary household contents." It's likely that you'll need to add a rider specifically covering your collection. A separate policy is another option.

There are companies that specialize in collectibles insurance; they are frequently less expensive, and some authorities recommend these policies. Collectors' clubs are often able to offer group rates to members—another good reason to join. The ANA offers policies to its members.

The Half Eagle ($5 gold coin) designed by Bela Lyon Pratt, issued 1908–29, departs from previous U.S. circulating-coin designs in that the device areas in raised relief are depressed below the surrounding field surfaces. This example was minted in 1909. *Photo courtesy of Bowers and Merena Galleries.*

LIVING WITH YOUR COLLECTION

Very few collectors display their coins openly, except perhaps a favorite coin with sentimental significance or a proof set that lends itself to framed display. Even a coin album among other volumes in a bookcase is more of a signal that valuable coins are about than most collectors want to convey. Most people keep their collections in closed areas—locked cabinets or file drawers at the least, home safes or strongboxes ideally—for two reasons: security and preservation.

Many experts advise that you shouldn't keep valuable coins anywhere in your home. The best place for them is a safe-deposit box at your bank. Still, among trusted colleagues in the hobby, as well as family and close friends, the ardent collector will want to show off his coins, or at least a few key pieces. The guiding principle here is trust. Don't show your coins to just anybody, don't leave even a modestly valuable coin folder or album lying in plain sight, and don't talk openly in public places about your collection.

If you keep your collection at home, it should be under lock and key at all times when you're not handling it. The best place is a home safe firmly bolted to the floor of a closet.

COLLECTOR'S COMPASS

TM

Even a secured home safe is not the ideal environment for storing valuable coins. Most home safes are designed to be fireproof, and accomplish this by sandwiching a layer of moisture in their walls. This moisture can cause surface detractions to coins if it seeps into the safe. Therefore, if you use a fireproof safe, be sure to add packages of desiccant silica gel to the interior. You may be able to pick some up without charge at your local consumer-electronics store. Every two to three months, remove the packets and put them in the oven at a low temperature (200 to 225 degrees) for fifteen to twenty minutes. This evaporates the accumulated moisture, and the packets can be used repeatedly this way.

If you choose to store your collection in a safe-deposit box at your bank, have a discreet conversation with a bank vice president beforehand to determine if the bank's vault is climate controlled to avoid extremes of temperature and humidity.

Assuming that you observe these protective measures, having your coins where you can examine and appreciate them lends tremendous enjoyment to the hobby. You should spend time with your coins and a magnifying loupe, honing your grading skills. And as you look through your albums and holders, you'll most likely be inspired to acquire a library of books and magazines on coins. For many coin collectors, the hobby is a way to focus an interest in American history. Each coin has a story to tell, and once you begin researching the origins, designs, and minting of specific coins, you can go on and on.

While there's considerable gratification in spending time alone with your collection, once you've established a circle of trusted collector friends—through club membership, for instance—you'll find that sitting down together to "talk coins" can be an endlessly satisfying social pastime.

The Numismatic Roadshow

As your numismatic scholarship progresses, you may be moved to mount an exhibit at a coin show or a local institution such as a bank, library, or museum—assuming that security is adequate. Club shows—as well as ANA regional and national conventions—usually have a competition for exhibits, complete with awards. Exhibits and talks you may wish to give on your area of interest are a way to share your enthusiasm and knowledge, show off your collection, meet fellow collectors who share your passion, and perhaps gain new contacts and sources to help you build your collection.

Protecting Your Collection

Coin Folders and Albums

For the beginning collector of circulated coins, the best place to accumulate and protect your coins is coin folders or albums. These are available at coin shops and bookstores. With the advent of the State Quarters series, you'll find holders for these coins just about everywhere—discount, office-supply, and craft stores for starters. Blue Whitman coin folders have been familiar to collectors since the 1930s, but more recently, companies such as Harris have introduced flashier designs.

The Whitman coin folder

Folders are available for many series of modern U.S. coins. They're useful because there's a labeled slot for each known coin in the series—including all years and mint marks. It's easy to see what you're missing from a series you're building—although a few of those slots may remain empty for a long time, until you're ready to spring for a big-ticket coin.

The disadvantage to coin folders is that the reverses are covered: once you've pressed a coin in place, it's impossible to see the other side without removing it from the folder. Albums with die-cut leaves allow you to view your coins on both sides. Newer designs feature acetate sheets that slide in channels between the die-cut cardboard core and the surface material bonded to either side of it. You remove the acetate from one side to insert your coins, then slide it back in place, thus protecting the coins from rubbing against other leaves in the album. Take great care when

The Harris coin folder

inserting the acetate sheets, so as not to scratch the coins in their slots.

Another disadvantage of cardboard folders is that coins must be full-diameter to be held securely. Heavily worn coins will be slightly smaller than uncirculated or lightly circulated coins; they may fall out of the die-cut slot when you handle the folder.

Single-coin 2 x 2 holders

Single coins can be stored and displayed in cardboard and acetate fold-over windows, called 2 X 2s. Some are self-adhesive, so once the coin is enclosed it's pretty permanent. You can take the coin out only by tearing the 2 X 2 open.

Other designs require you to staple the holder closed. Usually, three staples—one on each of the open sides—will suffice. Experts counsel you to position the staples well back from the edge of the coin and press the ends of the staples down firmly so other coins can't be scratched inadvertently. Most important, if you decide to remove the coin, be sure to remove all the staples first. Many a valuable coin has been needlessly marred by a protruding staple point. Check your stapled 2 X 2s regularly to make sure that the staples are not beginning to rust; if they are, carefully remove your coins from the holders and repackage them in another type of container—a triacetate or Lucite holder, for instance.

Polyethylene "flips"

Mylar "flips" are clear plastic fold-over pockets that have become popular for single-coin storage. Our one caution is that Mylar is rather stiff and can scratch a coin: exercise great care when placing a coin in the flip or removing it. A softer, more pliant flip is made of polyethylene plastic, which is safe for long-term storage.

Flips made of polyvinyl chloride (PVC) are still circulating in the marketplace. Avoid them! PVC contains chemicals that are reactive with metal alloys—especially those containing copper. A coin left in a PVC holder over a long period is likely to become caked with a greenish, gooey deposit that's nearly impossible to remove, and the coin's value will be destroyed.

Paper coin envelopes have long been a favorite way to store single coins. You can write notes and identifying information on the outside, and the coin is safely stored inside. But wait! Make sure you use only acid-free coin envelopes. Many types of paper contain compounds of sulfuric acid that can splotch and darken coin surfaces. Acid-free envelopes are generally available from your coin dealer.

Koin-Tains in two sizes

If you collect standard denominations, a relatively new product—Koin-Tains—may be to your liking. These two-piece shells are made of triacetate, a clear, hard plastic. They slip over both sides of the coin and hold it in place by the rim. The sizes are limited, but to show favorite coins to advantage, Koin-Tains are a real plus. Another safe product—a three-piece sandwich held together with plastic screws—is made by Capital Plastics in Lucite. It's available for single coins and a number of kinds of sets.

Capital Plastics Lucite sandwich for $5 gold piece

Coin dealers also carry polyethylene or polystyrene tubes for storing rolls of coins.

COLLECTOR'S COMPASS

Don't rummage through your kitchen drawers and medicine cabinet for materials to store and display coins. Plastic pill bottles, plastic wrap, tissue paper, aluminum foil, and other materials all present hazards to preservation. The best policy is to buy your coin storage and display materials from a reputable coin dealer.

Long-Term Storage

Ideally, your coin collection should be stored in a climate that's similar to the one you'd like yourself—a room temperature of 65–70 degrees and relatively low humidity. Temperature extremes in and of themselves are not necessarily harmful to coins. But when taken from low temperatures to higher ones, coins can collect harmful condensation on their surfaces. Don't store coins in areas subject to dramatic swings in temperature, such as attics, basements, and garages. Avoid all areas subject to high humidity—bathrooms, laundry rooms, and kitchens lead the list.

A polystyrene tube

Capital Plastics Lucite sandwich for a 1999 State Quarters set

Keeping your coins in airtight triacetate or Lucite containers is one way to reduce exposure to airborne pollutants and humidity. If you're not storing them in airtight containers, add packets of desiccant silica gel and refresh them regularly. Otherwise, the airtight containers discussed above—but not folders or albums—will adequately protect your coins from airborne pollutants, such as tobacco smoke and cooking grease. Needless to say, you shouldn't smoke around valuable coins when they're out of their containers, nor expose coins to airborne pollutants for extended periods.

Although you need a strong incandescent or high-intensity light source to examine your coins with a magnifying loupe, under all other circumstances your coins should not be in direct light of any kind.

To Clean or Not to Clean

Expert upon expert will tell a beginning coin collector: Do not clean your coins. Period.

There are myriad cleaning methods that you may hear touted on the Internet, by other collectors, in books, or even by dealers. All have the potential to detract from, or even destroy, the coin's value. Common techniques range from scrubbing with a toothbrush (or worse, a wire brush!) to rubbing with a pencil eraser. The natural patina that an uncirculated coin has acquired is the result of its entire life span since leaving the mint. Once disturbed or removed, it will take years to reacquire.

Circulated coins may be so encrusted with dirt, grime, and grease that the temptation to improve their appearance is irresistible. So, knowing that you're taking a risk, if you're determined to clean them anyway, we'll at least give you a couple of relatively safe options. If you must satisfy your curiosity, try these treatments on coins that have next to no collectible value.

- **Mild soap and water.** A basin of warm water and mild liquid soap (not laundry detergent), such as Ivory, will remove superficial dirt and oils effectively. Wash coins singly in a basin with a cloth at the bottom to cushion them if they should fall. Wipe the coins with a soft cloth and dry them immediately after rinsing to avoid water spots (especially copper coins).

- **Olive oil.** You may want to try soaking grimy coins in a bath of olive oil for several hours. The oil will often soften grease and dirt accumulation. You can wipe the coins with a soft cloth, followed by the soap-and-water treatment described above. Don't be tempted to use even a soft brush to tease out stubborn particles. It will leave near-microscopic scratches that will detract from the coin's value and appeal.

- **Ultrasonic cleaner.** You may use an ultrasonic cleaner with a mild-soap-and-water solution to similar effect. Clean coins one at a time, placing a layer of soft cloth at the bottom of the cleaning reservoir to avoid damaging the coin.

There are several cleaning solutions made for dipping coins. These are acid-based and actually remove a microscopic layer of metal from the surfaces of a coin. Used properly by an experienced numismatist, dipping can make a coin shinier, but that's not the same as restoring its original luster. Used repeatedly or improperly, acid dips can seriously damage details.

Sacrifice Some Coins in the Name of Research
You may want to "destroy" some almost worthless coins by rubbing them with a pencil eraser, abrasive cleanser, metal polish, steel-wool soap pad, or toothbrush and toothpaste. Label each example of an improper cleaning method, and keep the coins for study. You may be able to spot evidence of destructive cleaning more readily among the coins you examine in the marketplace after you've created some examples of your own.

A Coronet (or Liberty Head) Eagle ($10 gold coin), issued 1838–1907.

Photos courtesy of Bowers and Merena Galleries.

IF AND WHEN YOU DECIDE TO SELL

As great as your passion for U.S. coins may be, the day may come when you want or need to sell some or all of your holdings. When you do, there are a variety of ways to go about it—some quicker than others, some more work than others, and some more likely to be profitable.

Options for Selling Part or All of a Collection

Whatever your reason for selling, here's where good record keeping pays off. If you have every coin described in a database or a set of inventory forms, it will be easy to review what you have to sell. Being able to reference what you paid will help you to set prices. If you took care to capture the details of each coin's condition and detractions, you've already gone a long way toward stating a grade for the coin and writing a comprehensive description.

Selling to a Fellow Collector

You may have developed a collecting friendship with someone who you know would love to own some or all of the coins in your collection. He'll likely want to bargain with you, but even so, this kind of sale will probably bring you closer to retail value than selling to a dealer.

COLLECTOR'S COMPASS ™

The Added Value of Sets and High-Grade Key Coins

When it comes time to sell, a dealer will be looking at your set for completeness and condition. If one or more key coins are missing, the value will be greatly diminished.

There is a market for complete sets or series in a high and/or uniform grade. If you've built one and want to sell it, you're much better off taking it to auction than selling to a dealer.

If you've got the key coins in the upper grades of About Uncirculated or Mint State quality, consider having them professionally graded, which costs about $30 per coin. Once slabbed by a reputable grading service, there's a good chance you'll sell them at top retail value on your own. And you may get lucky and have one or more coins slide up a point in grade from where you thought they would be, significantly increasing their potential value.

Selling Your Entire Collection to a Dealer

This option will probably net you the lowest return on money invested, as dealers only pay a percentage of current market value. Take the time to go through your collection item by item and determine what you think each coin or set is worth. Our experts advise against hawking your collection to every dealer in the area. Word gets out quickly, and dealers tend to devalue a collection they know has been shopped around. Be selective and seek out the dealers who share your specialty and appreciate what you've collected; they will be more likely to pay you a good price because they know how to turn the coins over quickly to other interested parties.

Consigning Your Coins with a Dealer

Overall, consignment is a fairly dicey way to liquidate your collection, unless you have implicit trust and a long-standing relationship with the dealer. On the upside, you get the benefit of the dealer's market network and exposure—connections with other dealers, a retail-shop presence, coin-show exhibits, perhaps a Web dealership. But a consigning dealer may undergrade your coins in order to stimulate quick sale. Or he may accept them in the hope that, after a period of lackluster sales activity, you'll sell the collection to him outright, at a wholesale price.

If you decide to consign your collection, pay close attention to the details of the agreement before you sign.

Selling Your Coins in Online Auctions

These days, the big online auctions are the most popular venue for a self-seller. But there are some pros and cons—in addition to the work needed to get your listings up.

On the plus side, you're putting your offerings before a huge audience. And if you have any rarities or highly desirable coins, it only takes two people desperate to add that key coin to their collections to drive the bidding beyond what you could hope to realize from most other sources.

On the downside, your more common coins may go unsold, even after multiple listings and with no reserve prices. You may have to sell them by some other means for little more than their bullion (or "melt") value.

The All-Important Description

Whether you decide to try to sell online or through ads in the numismatic magazines and trade papers, your description is all-important. Remember that if your description does not match the item, the buyer will quite correctly demand a refund of both the purchase price and any postage and insurance that he paid. Here's a good example for reference:

1917 Walking Liberty Half PCGS MS-64

Sharp strike with smooth fields and light rose toning. Super coin that is as nice as most offered as MS-65. Current PCGS slab. Buyer pays shipping and handling: $5.00 domestic; $15 international via Global Priority.

Photos should show both sides of the slabbed coin with all details of the professional grading visible.

Selling at Auction

There are many issues involved in selling collectible coins at auction. Read *The Coin Collector's Survival Manual,* revised fourth edition (Bonus Books, 2000), Chapter 11, for a full discussion. The author, Scott A. Travers, is a high-profile consumer advocate for the coin-buying public.

A Great Starter for a Mint-State Collection:
The Jefferson Nickel Five-Cent Piece

Originally, America used silver half-dimes as five-cent pieces. In 1866 the first nickel-alloy five-cent pieces were authorized, and since then we've had only four basic designs: the Shield, the Liberty Head, the Buffalo, and the Jefferson. The Jefferson five-cent coin was released in 1938, after a national contest for the obverse and reverse designs. Currently, the Jefferson nickel is widely available in MS-60 and higher specimens at reasonable prices. Although a few key coins in the series are valued in the hundreds of dollars, many MS-63 and even MS-65 coins can be purchased for under $10. A distinguishing characteristic often mentioned in descriptions of these coins is "full steps," referring to the quality of the strike evident in the five (sometimes six) steps visible on the porch of Monticello on the reverse; on lesser-grade coins, these steps may be indistinct.

Photos courtesy of Rare Coin Galleries of Seattle, Inc.

Your Collection as a Bequest

The pleasure—and work—of a lifetime of collecting coins can be a meaningful bequest to your descendants. Ultimately, someone else will decide what happens to your collection, how it's eventually sold, and for what purpose. But your gift will still be remembered—and valued—as it contributed to a college education, the down payment on a new house, a first car, or some other worthwhile purchase. If you choose this route rather than outright liquidation, be sure to pass on all the documentation you've accumulated with the collection itself.

Dealing with Life's Other Certainty

Regardless of the way you determine to part with your coin collection, be sure to consult with your tax professional beforehand as you weigh the alternatives. Collectible coins are defined as capital assets, and the gain or loss you realize in selling them has tax implications. Bequests over a certain value may also be subject to taxation, and you may be compelled to get a professional appraisal. Diligent record keeping really pays off at this point.

RESOURCES TO FURTHER YOUR COLLECTING

Shows

The number of coin shows held each year in the United States alone reaches well into the hundreds. The easiest access to locations, dates, and venues is the state-by-state online directory found at www.coinclub.com/shows. Also, separate directories are maintained for Canadian and other international shows.

As show dates become firm throughout the year, the entries are often hyperlinked to clubs' or promoters' sites, which give full information on each show. Listings include ANA-affiliated shows, club shows, and commercially promoted shows.

If you don't own a personal computer, almost all public libraries provide online research services. You can go to the Web site, select the states that are within striking distance, and print out all show schedules.

Dealers

The best place for a newcomer to start looking for reputable dealers is at the American Numismatic Association Web site, with its state-by-state dealer listing. (Again, your public library can provide online access if you don't own a computer.) Go to www.money.org, then click on "Marketplace Dealers." This link will take you to the ANA list of dealers who are supposed to subscribe to its code of ethics. You can search listings alphabetically, by specialty, or by state.

Another good starting point is the Professional Numismatists Guild Web site at www.pngdealers.com. PNG is a professional dealer organization founded in 1955. It numbers more than two hundred members nationwide who subscribe to a code of ethics. The guild publishes a free directory of its membership that also features collecting information and guidelines for newcomers (request by telephone, mail, or e-mail). The Web site includes a member dealer directory, searchable by name and by name within state.

Professional Numismatists Guild
3950 Concordia Lane
Fallbrook, CA 92028
Telephone: 760-728-1300
Fax: 760-728-8507
E-mail: info@pngdealers.com

Many of the coins featured in this book came from:
Rare Coin Galleries of Seattle, Inc.
1521 Third Avenue South
Seattle, WA 98134-1527
Telephone: 206-624-4440 *or* 800-774-7557

Auctions

These are the premier houses which specialize in numismatic auctions and sales, and their minimums for handling collections on consignment may be high ($5,000 estimated value, or more).

Bowers and Merena Galleries
P.O. Box 1224
Wolfeboro, NH 03894-1224
Telephone: 800-458-4646 *or* 603-569-5095
Fax: 603-569-5319
Web site: www.bowersandmerena.com
One of the foremost numismatic auction houses in the country. Check the Web site for schedule of upcoming auctions, many held in association with major coin shows nationwide.

Heritage Numismatic Auctions, Inc.
100 Highland Park Village, Suite 200
Dallas, TX 75205-2788
Telephone: 800-US-COINS (872-6467) *or* 214-528-3500
Web site: www.heritagecoins.com
Heritage handles a large volume of high-grade coins at live auctions held nationwide in conjunction with major coin shows, as well as via online auctions and fixed-price sales.

Malter Galleries Inc.
17005 Ventura Boulevard
Encino, CA 91316
Telephone: 888-784-2131 *or* 818-784-7772
Fax: 818-784-4726
Web site: www.maltergalleries.com
Conducts live auctions, as well as online auctions.

Stack's Rare Coins
123 West 57th Street
New York, NY 10019
Telephone: 212-582-2580
Fax: 212-245-5018 *or* 212-582-1946
Web site: www.stacks.com
One of the oldest and most prestigious auction houses and dealerships—dating
    back to 1933. Stack's has conducted more than 600 public and mail-bid
    auctions since its founding. Harvey G. Stack analyzed the U.S. Treasury's
    commemorative coin programs and recommended the concept that became the
    State Quarters series.

Superior Galleries
9478 West Olympic Boulevard
Beverly Hills, CA 90212-4246
Telephone: 800-421-0754 *or* 310-203-9855
Fax: 310-203-0496
Web site: www.superiorsc.com
Superior conducts live auctions at the Long Beach, California, coin shows
    throughout the year. For the past two years, it has been the official auctioneer
    of the ANA National Convention.

Numismatic Publications

COINage
Miller Magazines, Inc.
4880 Market Street
Ventura, CA 93003-7783
Telephone: 805-644-3824
Web site: www.coinagemag.com
Published monthly. Miller also publishes an annual, *Quarter Collector,* of particular
    interest to State Quarters collectors.

The Coin Dealer Newsletter (the Greysheet)
The Certified Coin Dealer Newsletter (the Bluesheet)
P.O. Box 7939
Torrance, CA 90504
Telephone: 310-515-7369
Fax: 310-515-7534
Web site: www.greysheet.com
These weekly newsletters are widely considered the standards among dealers for
    up-to-date price guidance. The Greysheet covers nearly every U.S. coin issued;
    valuations reference coins that have not been professionally graded. The
    counterpart Bluesheet provides current values for graded—or slabbed—coins.
    These newsletters are not cheap, but short-term subscriptions are available; you
    can sample them at minimal cost to assess their usefulness.

Coins Magazine

Krause Publications, Inc.
700 East State Street
Iola, WI 54990-0001
Telephone: 800-258-0929 (subscription services) *or* 715-445-2214
Web site: www.krause.com
Published monthly.

Coin World

Amos Press
P.O. Box 150
Sidney, OH 45365-0150
Telephone: 800-253-4555 (subscription services) *or* 937-498-0800
Fax: 937-498-0812
Web site: www.coinworld.com
Published weekly. Includes "Trends of U.S. Coins" with current values for more
than fifty thousand coins in twelve grades.

Numismatic News

Krause Publications
700 East State Street
Iola, WI 54990-0001
Telephone: 800-258-0929 (subscription services) *or* 715-445-2214
Web site: www.krause.com
A weekly tabloid that also includes a monthly price guide (*Coin Market*) as part of
the subscription.

The Numismatist

The American Numismatic Association
818 North Cascade Avenue
Colorado Springs, CO 80903-3279
Telephone: 719-632-2646
Fax: 719-634-4085
Web site: www.money.org
This monthly magazine is a benefit of ANA membership.

Clubs and Associations

The American Numismatic Association Web site, at www.money.org, features a state-by-
state listing of ANA-affiliated clubs, as well as national, regional, international, and
specialty clubs. Click on "Club Listings" to get to the club front page. There you'll
also find a link to ANA regional coordinators. The one in your area will be happy to
tell you all he can about local clubs—both ANA-affiliated and others.

Bill Fivaz's delightful book *Helpful Hints for Enjoying Coin Collecting* (see
"Bibliography and Recommended Reading" on page 123), includes an extensive
listing of clubs devoted to specialized coin-collecting interests. Many of these clubs
maintain their own Web sites. Below is just a sampling of the range of interests
represented.

Barber Coin Collectors' Society
415 Ellen Drive
Brookhaven, MS 39601
Web site: http://www.geocities.com/Eureka/Concourse/4920/bccs.htm
Enthusiasts of coins designed by Charles Barber.

Civil War Token Society
26548 Mazur Dr.
Rancho Palos Verdes, CA 90275
Web site: home.att.net/~cwts/cwts.htm
More than 1,000 members who collect store cards, sutler tokens, and patriotic Civil
   War tokens. Publishes a quarterly journal. Visit the Web site to learn more
   about this fascinating specialty.

**Combined Organizations of Numismatic Error
   Collectors of America (CONECA)**
9017 Topperwind Court
Fort Worth, TX 76134-5501
Web site: http://hermes.csd.net/~coneca
Enthusiasts of all kinds of mint errors.

Early American Coppers Club
P.O. Box 15782
Cincinnati, OH 45215
Web site: www.eacs.org
Serious collectors of Large Cents and other copper coins.

The Elongated Collectors
P.O. Box 161
Fenton, MI 48430
Web site: www.money.org/clubs/tec.html

The Lincoln Cent Society
P.O. Box 113
Winfield, IL 60190

Love Token Society
P.O. Box 970
Mandeville, LA 70470
Web site: www.lovetokensociety.homepage.com

The Numismatic Bibliomania Society
P.O. Box 6885
Lawrenceville, NJ 08648
Web site: www.coinbooks.org
Devoted to the literature of numismatics.

Original Hobo Nickel Society
P.O. Box 38669
Colorado Springs, CO 80937

Society of Silver Dollar Collectors
P.O. Box 2123
North Hills, CA 91393-0123
Web site: www.vamlink.com

Society for U.S. Commemorative Coins
P.O. Box 3637
Thousand Oaks, CA 91359-3637
Web site: www.money.org/sum-carmody.html

Token and Medal Society (TAMS)
P.O. Box 832854
Miami, FL 33283
Web site: www.angelfire.com/id/TAMS
The primary exonumia collectors' association. Publishes the *TAMS Journal* (a
bimonthly magazine), maintains a lending library for members (for the cost of
postage), and publishes an extensive program of reference books on tokens,
medals, and other exonumic categories.

Young Numismatists of America
c/o American Numismatic Association
818 North Cascade Avenue
Colorado Springs, CO 80903-3279
Web site: www.money.org

Online Auctions and Marketers

This category increasingly includes the major dealerships and auction houses as they
develop Web marketing presences; thus, you should visit the Web sites of the auction
houses listed above, as well as the Web sites listed below. In addition to
www.eBay.com, which typically features in the neighborhood of fifty thousand U.S.
coins for auction at any given time, a newcomer should visit the following two sites,
if only to see the scans posted there to learn more about coins, their conditions, and
their values. As with eBay, you have to register to participate in the auctions.

www.certifiedcoinexchange.com
This Houston-based firm offers professional numismatic information services, including up-to-the-moment pricing information on investment-grade coins, to the trade by
subscription. But the site also maintains an auction service for dealer-to-buyer transactions at www.cce-auction.com. You need to register and abide by cce-auction rules.
Keep in mind that any purchases you make are between you and the individual seller, not cce-auction. There is no buyer's fee on this auction site.

www.teletrade.com
Teletrade.com is the coin division of Greg Manning Auctions, based in West Caldwell, New Jersey, an international collectibles mail-phone-Internet auction service. Here you bid on the basis of descriptions and scans of professionally certified and slabbed coins. While cce-auction.com operates as a clearinghouse for seller-to-buyer transactions, teletrade.com is a true auction house: it takes possession of the lots, collects payments from winning bidders, and handles shipping. Teletrade charges a buyer's fee, based on the price paid for the lot. There is also a guaranteed return period, but rules are detailed and stringent.

Museums

The American Numismatic Society
Broadway at 155th Street
New York, NY 10032
Telephone: 212-234-3130
Fax: 212-234-3381
E-mail: info@amnumsoc.org
Web site: www.amnumsoc.org
The A.N.S. collection numbers nearly one million coins, and the research
    library contains more than one hundred thousand items. This is the oldest
    numismatic organization in the U.S., and while the public exhibits are open to
    any interested parties, you must be a member and have a serious research
    purpose to be granted access to the larger holdings.

Robert H. Gore Jr. Collection
University of Notre Dame Libraries
Department of Special Collections
102 Hesburgh Library
Notre Dame, IN 46556
Telephone: 219-631-5636
E-mail: Louis.E.Jordan.1@nd.edu
One of the foremost collections of Colonial and state coinage. Contact the curator
    for application requirements to view the collection, which is held for serious
    numismatic study. You can see a number of the coins by going to the site of
    the National Numismatic Collection of the Smithsonian Institution
    (http://americanhistory.si.edu/csr/cadnnc.htm), clicking on the link "Other
    Sites of Interest," and finding the Gore collection.

The Money Museum, American Numismatic Association
818 North Cascade Avenue
Colorado Springs, CO 80903-3279
Telephone: 719-632-2646
Web site: www.money.org
The ANA's Money Museum mounts ongoing exhibits in its headquarters on the
    Colorado College campus, as well as touring exhibits and online exhibits. The
    ANA's educational programs are scheduled year-round and you may view the
    course catalog from the Web site.

The Smithsonian Institution
Smithsonian Information
SI Building, Room 153
Washington, DC 20560-0010
Telephone: 202-357-2700
Web site: www.si.edu
The National Museum of American History holds the National Numismatic
Collection in its Hall of Money. With more than 400,000 coins and over
550,000 pieces of currency, the collection is centered around contributions
over the years from the U.S. Mint, as well as from the collections of Josiah K.
Lilly and Willis H. duPont (Russian coins), among others.

Historic Sites

United States Mint
Tour Information
Web site: www.usmint.gov
Tours of the main mint in Philadelphia, as well as the Denver branch, are given
free. Call the respective location or visit the U.S. Mint Web site for details.

Philadelphia:
151 North Independence Mall East
Philadelphia, PA 19106-1886
Telephone: 215-408-0114

Denver:
320 West Colfax Avenue
Denver, CO 80204-2693
Telephone: 303-405-4761

Libraries

The American Numismatic Association maintains an extensive lending library for
research and use by its members. The American Numismatic Society library is open
to the public and for use by members; the library also handles some thirty thousand
research requests per year by mail and e-mail. You may search the ANS database from
the Web site at www.amnumsoc.org.

Grading Services

Grading services are listed here together with their abbreviations and acronyms, as
you'll see them in listings and ads for certified and slabbed coins. While some will deal
directly with individuals, most operate through coin retailers. The fee to grade a coin
varies, determined in most instances by speed of turnaround. Below is a selection of
the most prominent from the twenty-plus grading services currently active. For a
complete and detailed set of profiles on grading services and their histories, go to the
Web site for the World Internet Numismatic Society (www.winsociety.org), click on
the "Newsletter" tool button, and then enter "Grading Services" in the search box.

Amos Certification Service, Inc. (ANACS)
P.O. Box 182141
Columbus, OH 43218-2141
Telephone: 800-888-1861
Web site: www.anacs.com
This grading service was operated by the ANA beginning in 1979 as the American
Numismatic Association Certification Service (thus the retained initials) until it
was sold to Amos Press in 1990.

Independent Coin Grading Company (ICG)
Market Center DTC
7901 East Belleview Avenue, Suite 50
Englewood, CO 80111
Telephone: 877-221-4424 *or* 303-221-4424
Fax: 303-221-5524
Web site: www.icgcoin.com

Numismatic Guaranty Corporation of America (NGC)
P.O. Box 1776
Parsippany, NJ 07054
Web site: www.ngccoin.com
The official independent grading service of the American Numismatic Association.
Individuals must submit coins for grading through one of 1,300 ANA-certified
dealers. You can find a certified dealer in your area via either the ANA or NGC
Web site.

Professional Coin Grading Service (PCGS)
P.O. Box 9458
Newport Beach, CA 92658
Telephone: 800-447-8848 *or* 949-833-0600
Web site: www.pcgs.com
PCGS accepts coins for grading from individuals who have joined its fee-based
membership program.

REPRESENTATIVE VALUE GUIDE

This highly selective sampling of coin values provides the newcomer with a sense of the some-times dramatic differences in prices for coins of progressively higher grades. Where no prices appear for the lower grades, the coin is generally not sold on the collector market or is valued only at the prevailing bullion price (pre-1965 silver coins). Where no prices appear in the Mint State (MS) columns, the coin is of such rarity in these grades as to be priced only on the infre-quent occasions when an example is sold publicly. Dates in boldface (with mint mark, where applicable) signify coins that are considered "key" in a series or type.

Values were compiled from multiple sources which our experts regard as reliable, providing an accurate "snapshot" of the market at the time of publication. However, this guide is intended only to help you develop a sense of comparative values. Reliable up-to-date resources should be consulted when considering any purchase. Individual price guides almost always list a single price per coin for each grade, whereas we have listed a range derived from multiple sources.

	VG-8	VF-20	EF-40	MS-60	MS-65
HALF-CENT					
1793	2,100–2,350	5,000–5,200	9,500–10,750		
1804 (Stemless Wreath)	40–42	90–105	200–265		
1832 (Classic Head)	25–32	50–55	70–90	205–225	
1853 (Coronet)	29–35	50–55	65–75	180–200	
LARGE CENT					
1793 (Wreath, lettered edge)					
	1,200–1,400	4,000–4,150	8,000–9,250		
1803 (small date, small fraction)					
	50–57.50	250–255	675–700		
1808	70–120	475–525	1,000–1,750		
1819 (large or small date)	14–22	55–60	100–150	275–300	
1834 (large 8, small stars, medium letters)					
	13.50–14	55–56	110–205	250–325	
1845	11–12	18–21	62.50–65	150–225	
1857 (large date)	30–32	50–55	75–95	275–390	
SMALL CENT (FLYING EAGLE)					
1857	18–19	33–36	85–100	220–250	2,550–3,750
SMALL CENT (INDIAN HEAD)					
1862	6–9	11–12	23–25	85–95	750–900
1872	70–90	275	325–350	450–550	
1877	500–575	850–900	1,250–1,375	2,000–2,150	
1887	1.50–1.80	3.75–5.50	13–14	32–40	
1900	1.35–1.45	2.15–2.25	7–10	21–25	
1909S	265–275	340–375	400–410	485–500	
SMALL CENT (LINCOLN)					
1909S (VDB)	400–420	500–525	550–575	700–715	
1914	0.50–.80	3–4	8.50–9	35–50	
1914D	100–110	195–200	425–450	900–1,075	
1943 (steel)		.30	.40	.80–.85	4–4.50
1955 (double die)		450–475	550–575	1,300–1,450	22,750–23,000

REPRESENTATIVE VALUE GUIDE

	VG-8	VF-20	EF-40	MS-60	MS-65
FIVE CENT (BUFFALO)					
1916 (double die)	3,000–3,400	7,000–7,250	10,000–12,000	27,000–27,500	
1918D (8 over 7)	600–650	2,000–2,050	4,400–4,500	13,500–16,000	
1921S	35–36	350–360	675–725	1,350–1,500	
1929	.85–1	1.75	4.5–5	21–32	275–325
1937D (three-legged)	220–225	335–340	410–450	1,200–1,350	14,000–19,750
FIVE CENT (JEFFERSON)					
1942S (silver alloy)	.45–.70	.75–1.45	1.50–2	5–6	13–25
1951D	.30–.50	.20–.40	.30–.50	.65–1.45	2.65–3
1963				.15–.16	.55–.75
DIME (MERCURY/WINGED LIBERTY HEAD)					
1916D	700–750	1,500–1,600	2,400–2,500	4,750–5,450	14,750–15,500
1921D	60–70	230–250	460–500	1,000–1,100	2,800–2,900
1927	1.50–1.55	3.50–3.75	5–6	22–25	164–165
1942 (2 over 1)	275–300	360–400	400–450	1,450–1,950	6,850–9,800
DIME (ROOSEVELT)					
1946	*	*	60–.75	.75–1.05	2–4.75
1950 (S over D)	*	*	.75–1.25	7–9.50	22.50–23
1962D	*	*	.60	.60–.90	1–2.75
QUARTER-DOLLAR (STANDING LIBERTY)					
1916	1,500–2,000	2,450–2,500	3,000–3,150	5,250–5,500	14,000–14,200
1918	17–18	30–33	45–47	135–150	620–625
1923S	190–250	330–350	435–450	600–700	1,750–1,975
1927S	15–20	150–155	1,000–1,050	3,800–3,850	9,700–9,750
1930S	3.5–4.25	12.50–15	25–30	115–130	480–500
QUARTER-DOLLAR (WASHINGTON)					
1932	3–4	6–7.50	8–9	20–21	210–250
1932S	45–49	55–69	65–79	260–290	2,750–3,250
1947D	*	1.50–2	1.75–2.50	3.75–4	20–45
1964	*	1–1.50	1.20–1.75	1.55–1.75	3.50–15
HALF-DOLLAR (BARBER)					
1893	18–20	75–80	150–160	450–500	
1897S	120–125	375–425	650–700	1,200–1,250	
1906S	8–12	75–80	165–192	475–565	
1914	40–45	300–325	475–495	900–915	
HALF-DOLLAR (WALKING LIBERTY)					
1917	6–7	18–20	28–32	105–110	800–855
1921D	160–165	690–700	1,800–2,000	2,500–3,250	12,600–13,500
1938D	22–24	40–45	90–100	380–400	825–860
1947	2.50–3	4–4.25	7–8	30–35	140–145
HALF-DOLLAR (FRANKLIN)					
1948	*	3.5–4.25	4.25–5	11–15	65–85
1949S	*	4.5–6.25	10–11	45–48	145–210
1963	*	2–3	2.85–3.75	3.50–4	85–90

REPRESENTATIVE VALUE GUIDE

	VG-8	VF-20	EF-40	MS-60	MS-65
HALF-DOLLAR (KENNEDY)					
1964 (silver)	*	*	*	2.50–3	5–15
1965 (silver-clad)	*	*	*	1.20–2	1.75–13
1972 (copper-nickel clad)	*	*	*	1	1.25–15
1776–1976 (nickel-clad)	*	*	*	.90–1	.90–10
1776–1976S (silver-clad)	*	*	*	2–2.75	4–13
DOLLAR (MORGAN)					
1879O	10.50–12	11–13.50	13–15	25–65	3,050–3,300
1881CC	85–110	125–130	120–140	170–200	600–650
1889CC	225–252	440–550	1,000–1,200	6,500–7,000	
1893S	950–1,100	1,900–2,100	4,000–4,550	30,000–37,500	260,000–285,000
1897	11.50–12	11–13	12–14	20–23	250–285
1903O	92.50–125	120–170	130–180	165–240	450–460
1904S	15–16	40–42	170–185	900–950	6,550–6,875
1921D	9–11	9.50–12	10–13	22–32	260–300
DOLLAR (PEACE)					
1921		42–44	50–53	130–145	2,650–2,750
1923		9–9.50	10–11.25	14–17	110–135
1928		135–150	150–165	180–210	2,850–3,150
1934D		15–17	18–20	75–78	1,800–2,000
DOLLAR (EISENHOWER)					
1971D (copper-nickel-clad)			1.15–1.50	2–2.50	21–32
1973S (silver-clad)			3–4	4–5	10–13
1776–1976 (copper-nickel-clad, low-relief Var. 1)				1.50–2	
DOLLAR (SUSAN B. ANTHONY)					
1979D				1.25–1.30	10–22
1981S				2.75–6	40–65
GOLD QUARTER-EAGLE ($2.50)					
1888 (Liberty)		160–180	195–200	450–500	
1910 (Indian)		130–135	150–155	240–265	4,750–5,200
GOLD HALF-EAGLE ($5.00)					
1873S (Liberty)		600–675	975–1,350	18,000–21,000	
1912 (Indian)		185–190	200–225	310–340	13,440–14,500
GOLD EAGLE ($10.00)					
1884S (Liberty)		210–250	230–270	550–650	
1909 (Indian)		300–310	350–380	510–525	8,440–8,900
GOLD DOUBLE EAGLE ($20.00)					
1896 (Liberty)		425–460	450–480	525–550	
1914 (Saint-Gaudens)		425–445	450–460	550–615	12,000–13,750

*Lesser grade coins valued at bullion prices only

BIBLIOGRAPHY AND
RECOMMENDED READING

Breen, Walter H. *Walter Breen's Complete Encyclopedia of U.S. and Colonial Coins.* New York: Doubleday, 1988.

Weighing in at 754 pages and with more than four thousand photos, this book is the cornerstone of many numismatists' reference libraries. Our experts agree it is the best single book to own from the beginning of your collecting. Still in print, its hefty price will put your adherence to our Golden Rule No. 2 to the test. Used copies may sometimes be found on the Web sites www.abe.com, www.alibris.com, and other out-of-print and rare-book services for somewhat less.

Bressett, Kenneth, and Abe Kosoff, eds. *Official A.N.A. Grading Standards for United States Coins.* 5th ed. Colorado Springs: American Numismatic Association, 1996.

An indispensable, authoritative guide for learning key grading points for each type of U.S. coin.

Fivaz, Bill. *Helpful Hints for Enjoying Coin Collecting.* Savannah, Ga.: Stanton Printing and Publishing, 1999.

A lively, down-to-earth how-to for new collectors, written by a lifelong numismatist who obviously loves the hobby.

Gibbs, William T., ed. *Coin World Guide to U.S. Coins, Prices, and Value Trends, 2001.* 13th ed. Sidney, Ohio: Amos Press, 2000.

Value guidance for individual coins (in up to ten grades), a fact-filled technical synopsis for each coin type, and numerous background essays on a variety of numismatic topics.

Herbert, Alan. *Coin Clinic: 1,001 Frequently Asked Questions.* Iola, Wis.: Krause Publications, 1995.

A compilation of Herbert's popular column in *Numismatic News.* While not an essential reference for new collectors, this is a fascinating read and gives an omnibus picture of the quirky, wonderful facts, anecdotes, trivia, and lore that spark the interests of coin collectors.

Reed, Brad, ed. *Coin World Comprehensive Catalog and Encyclopedia of United States Coins.* 2d ed. Sidney, Ohio: Amos Press, 1998.

Combines several of the features found in the Whitman Red Book with the strong points of *Coin World's* other publications. Contains more comprehensive technical information than the *Coin World Guide to U.S. Coins, Prices, and Value Trends,* more photos (though many are, unfortunately, muddy), and value listings for five grades.

Travers, Scott A. *The Coin Collector's Survival Manual.* Rev. 4th ed. Chicago: Bonus Books, 2000.

Travers has earned a reputation as the Ralph Nader of coin collecting, resulting from his many pro-consumer activities in the field. This is a great introductory book for newcomers, addressing just about every aspect of numismatics in a pointed, easy-to-understand format.

Yeoman, R. S. *The Official Red Book: A Guide Book of United States Coins.* 54th ed. New York: Whitman Coin Products (St. Martin's Press), 2000.

The most authoritative price guide among several on the market, offering values for up to six grades, as well as basic general information for all U.S. coins.

ABOUT THE INTERNATIONAL SOCIETY OF APPRAISERS

The Collector's Compass series is endorsed by the International Society of Appraisers, one of North America's leading nonprofit associations of professionally educated and certified personal-property appraisers. Members of the ISA include many of the industry's most respected independent appraisers, auctioneers, and dealers. ISA appraisers specialize in more than two hundred areas of expertise in four main specialty pathways: antiques and residential contents, fine art, gems and jewelry, and machinery and equipment.

Established in 1979 and consisting of more than 1,375 members, the ISA is founded on two core principles: to educate its members through a wide range of continuing education and training opportunities, and to promote and maintain the highest ethical and professional standards in the field of appraisals.

Education through the ISA

In conjunction with the University of Maryland University College, the ISA offers a series of post-secondary professional courses in appraisal studies, including a two-level certification program.

The ISA recognizes three membership levels within its organization— Associate Member, Accredited Member, and Certified Member—with educational programs in place for achieving higher distinctions within the society. ISA members who complete the required coursework are recognized with the title of Certified Appraiser of Personal Property (CAPP). Through its pioneering education programs, the ISA plays a vital role in producing qualified appraisers with a professional education in appraisal theory, principles, procedures, ethics, and law as it pertains to personal-property appraisal.

Professional Standards of the ISA

The ISA is dedicated to the highest ethical standards of conduct, ensuring public confidence in the ability and qualifications of its members. To help members perform their work with the most up-to-date knowledge of professional standards, the ISA is continually updating, expanding, and improving its courses and criteria of conduct.

For more information about the International Society of Appraisers, contact its corporate offices:

Toll-free: 800-472-4732
E-mail: ISAHQ@isa-appraisers.org
Web site: www.isa-appraisers.org

ABOUT THE CONTRIBUTORS

Leon Castner is president and head auctioneer of Castner's, a multi-discipline appraisal and auction firm with headquarters in Branchville, New Jersey, where he has handled numerous estate coin collections. He also serves as president of New Jersey Auctioneers and is a senior partner of National Appraisal Consultants, located in Hope, New Jersey. Mr. Castner holds a doctorate in valuation science, has taught many appraisal and antiques courses across the country, co-hosts the radio program *Trash or Treasure,* and writes for several magazines and Strauss newspapers. He lives in northwestern New Jersey with his wife and seven children.

Christopher J. Kuppig has spent his entire career in book publishing. For several years he directed programs at Dell Publishing, Consumer Reports Books, and most recently Chilton Book Company—where his assignments included managing the Wallace-Homestead and Warman's lines of antiques-and-collectibles guides.

In 1997, Mr. Kuppig founded Stone Studio Publishing Services, a general management consultancy to book publishers. Acting as series editor for the Collector's Compass series has given him the opportunity to draw upon his wide-ranging network of contacts in the collecting field.

Mr. Kuppig resides with his wife and three children in eastern Massachusetts.

O. L. Wallis has been active in numismatics for more than thirty years. He has served as president of the California State Numismatic Association, Northern California Numismatic Association, California Exonumist Society, Pacific Coast Numismatic Society, San Francisco Coin Club, and Vallejo Numismatic Society; he has also been a national exhibit judge for the American Numismatic Association. In 1984, he was named a Numismatic Ambassador by a panel of his peers in a national award program sponsored by *Numismatic News.* Mr. Wallis's collecting interests include the Official Presidential Inaugural Medals, Charles A. Lindbergh, and Admiral George Dewey.

During World War II, Mr. Wallis served as a U.S. Marine in the Battle for Okinawa. By profession he is a retired National Parks Service biologist and naturalist. He resides with his wife in San Rafael, California.

William B. Whetstone is a professional numismatist who specializes in American, Canadian, and ancient coins. As both a collector and a dealer for more than forty years, his personal interests are in Colonial tokens, eighteenth-century American issues, and Roman imperatorial coins.

Working as a professional appraiser, Mr. Whetstone was a director of the International Society of Appraisers for five years, and for two terms was the Society's president. Currently he is the managing partner of both Thompson & Whetstone Inc. (fine antiques) and Carsley, the oldest numismatic firm in Canada.

Educated at McGill University, where he took an honors degree in history, Mr. Whetstone has always been passionate about the study and collecting of historically important coins. He currently resides with his children and big black dog in the countryside west of Montreal, Quebec.

INDEX

Note: Page numbers in italics denote information in a photo, illustration, or caption.

A

alloys, 28–29, 30–31, 32–33, *61,* 80
copper–nickel, 12, 29, *30,* 53
alterations, 83–85
American Numismatic Association, 33, 34, 65, 92, 97, 114
beginners, 18, 38–39
Certification Service, 81
Anthony, Susan B., *61*
appraisals, 94–97
auctions, live, 14, 18, 65–66, 72–75, 91, 109, 112–113
See also Internet auctions

B

Barber, Charles, 9, 16, *16, 54, 64,* 90
books, 39, 123
Buffalo nickel. *See* five-cent pieces, Buffalo

C

cents, 28
Coronet, *14,* 50
elongated, 85
flying eagle, *51,* 71, 120
Fugio (Franklin), 28, 88
half-, 28, *29, 52,* 84
Hawaiian, *82*
Indian Head, 29, *51,* 71, *71,* 88, *89,* 120
Large, *50, 51, 71,* 120
Lincoln, 12, 25, 28, 31, 42, 120
Lincoln Memorial, *66,* 80
Lincoln Wheat Ears, *49,* 80, *80*
Small, 71, 120
cleaning, 83, 104–105
coin, anatomy of a, *9*

collectors' clubs, 18, 42, 114–116
commemorative coins, 15, 17, 20, *20,* 42, *58, 96*
condition, 10, 15, 72, 81
Congress, 20, 28, 33
design approval, 12, 32, *56*
silver dollars, *15, 60, 83*
copper, *30,* 30–31, 71, 82–83, 86
Coronet, 14, *26, 29, 50, 62, 106*
counterfeits, 80, 91–92

D

damage, 7, 11, 33–34, 37, 43, 69, *80,* 81–82
dealers, 15, 18–19, 39, 43–47, 72, 93–95, 111–112
learning from, 42, 65–68
selling to, 107–109
denominations, 28–29, *51*
designers, 9, 16, 31–32, 90
designs, 8, 28–29, 31–32, 86–87
dimes, 17, 28–29, 31, 84, 90
Winged Liberty Head, *34, 55,* 121
dollars, 20, *60, 61,* 122
Morgan, *15, 60,* 90
Peace, *60*
Sacagawea, 21, *61,* 87–88
See also silver dollars
Double Eagle, 8, *8,* 14, *26,* 31, *62,* 86–87, 91–92, 122

E

Eagle, *40, 62, 63, 106,* 122
eagles, 17, 28, *51*
engravers, 16, 31–32, 90

errors, 17–18, 32, *49, 59, 87,* 87–88, *89*

F

five-cent pieces, 28–29, *53*
Buffalo, 43, *54, 84,* 84–85, 121
Jefferson, 7, *87,* 110, *110,* 121
Liberty Head, *54*
Shield, *53, 54*
Franklin, Benjamin, *6,* 22, 28, *57*
Fugio. *See* cents

G

gold coins, 9, *26,* 28, *54, 62, 63, 98, 106,* 122
damage, 82
luster, 86
minting of, 30
by Saint-Gaudens, *8,* 31, *40,* 86–87
grading, 15, 24, *34,* 36–38, 81, 108
and auctions, 65, 72
and purchasing, 22–23, 46–47, 67–69
services, 42, 83, 85, 89–90, 96, 118–119

H

half-cents, 29, *29, 52,* 84, 120
half-dollars, *6,* 20, 22, 31, *57, 76,* 121–122
Half Eagle, *63, 98,* 122
handling coins, 10, 48, 77–79
history of coins, 18, 27–32
Hobo Nickels, *84,* 84–85

I

Indian Head cents. *See* cents, Indian Head

Indian Head Eagle. *See* Eagle
insurance, 93, 95, 97
Internet auctions, 19, 46, 68–70, 72, 97, 109, 116–117
inventory, 93–94, 107
investment potential, 20, 22, 35, 47

L

Liberty, 38, *54, 64,* 71, *71,* 87
  Draped Bust cents, *52*
  Head, *29, 54, 62,* 90, *106*
  Standing, quarter, *56*
  symbol of, 7, 17, 28, 31, *61*
  Walking, half-dollar, *57, 76*
  Winged Head, dime, *34, 55*
Lincoln, Abraham, 20, 28
  cents, 12, 25, 28, 31, 42
  Memorial cents, *66,* 80
  Wheat Ears cents, *49,* 80, *80*
Longacre, James, 16, 71
Love Tokens, 84
luster, 38, 68, 69, 86

M

mail-order purchasing, 47, 67
manufacturing process, 32–33
Mercury dimes. *See* Liberty, Winged Head, dime
metals, 30–31
mint branches, 30
  Denver, 12, 16, 88
  Philadelphia, *6,* 12, 16, *21,* 29, 30, 31, *40, 49,* 88
  San Francisco, 12, 16, *26,* 30, 31, 35
  See also U.S. Mint
mint marks, *6,* 9, 11, 16, 17, 30, 31, 88
Mint State coins, 37–38, 46, 68, 69, 81, 85–86

Morgan, George T., silver dollar, *15, 60,* 90
mottoes, 9, 12, 28–29
museums, 34, 72, 117–118

N

nickels. *See* five-cent pieces

O

online auctions. *See* Internet auctions

P

pennies. *See* cents
Pratt, Bela Lyon, *63, 98*
preservation, 33–34, 81
price guides, 18, 39, 41, 79
proof coins, 12, 35, *53*
proof sets, 15, 17, 35, *35*
publications, 18, *19,* 39, 113–114

Q

quarters, 28, 31, *56,* 84, 121
  Barber, *16, 64,* 90
  Bicentennial, 11, 20
  State. *See* State Quarters
  Washington, 11, 17, 20, *61,* 88, 121

R

rarity, 20, 27, 38, 47, *54,* 81
  and value, 22, 89–90
reale, 27, 29
record keeping, 43, 92–94

S

Sacagawea. *See* dollars, Sacagawea
Saint-Gaudens, Augustus, *8,* 9, 14, 31, *40, 63,* 86–87
  See also Double Eagle *and* Eagle
selling coins, 107–109
silver, 12, 38, 82, 86
silver dollars, 28, 37–38, 42, *51, 83*

commemorative, *20, 96*
  Morgan, *15, 60,* 90
slabbing, 34, 46–47, 67–68, 72
  and grading, 15, 22–23, 108
State Quarters, 11, 12–13, 35, *58–59*
  design, 12, 32
  holders for, 13, 101
  and new collectors, 17, 19, 21, 22
  storage, 10, 94, 99–104

T

terminology, 29
three-cent pieces, *30*
toning, 11, 38, 68–69, 86
two-cent pieces, *51*

U

U.S. Mint, 8, 15, 16, *21,* 28, 30, 34, 37, 89, 118
  and coin designs, 31–32
  and commemorative coins, 17, 20
  See also mint branches
U.S. Treasury Department, 12, 14, 28, 30–31, *61,* 71

V

value, 32, 35, 43, 85–91
  fluctuations in, 8, 21–25, 42

W

Washington, George, 20, 28
  quarters, 7, 11, 12, 17, *61,* 88
Web sites, 14, 66, 75, 112–118
  education, 19, 85, 91
  purchasing through, 45–47, 68–70, 72
  See also Internet auctions
whizzing, 43, 83
Winged Liberty Head dime. *See* dimes, Winged Liberty Head